EVANGELICALS –

THEN AND NOW

EVANGELICALS –
THEN AND NOW

by

Peter Jeffrey

 EVANGELICAL PRESS

EVANGELICAL PRESS
Faverdale North Industrial Estate, Darlington, DL3 0PH,
England.

Evangelical Press USA
P. O. Box 825, Webster, New York 14580, USA

e-mail: sales@evangelicalpress.org
web: http://www.evangelicalpress.org

First published 2004

British Library Cataloguing in Publication Data available

ISBN 0 85234 564 X

Printed and bound in Great Britain by CPD (Wales),
Ebbw Vale

INTRODUCTION

To reach the age of 65 is a milestone in the life of most folk. It is the age of retirement, the age when you become a pensioner. So it is a good time to look back and try and assess what has happened in local church life over the past 40 years.

I am not looking back with nostalgia, wishing for a return of 'the good old days.' I hope I have enough sense to realise that not everything old is good, even as not everything new is bad. But I have to admit that in recent years I have had to pull myself up for thinking like an old man. The old man's thoughts go something like this – the younger preachers are not as good as the older ones and there is not the commitment in the church today like there use to be. If you think like an old man, you will act like an old man, and personally, at 65, I don't think of myself as old. It is true that very often my body contradicts this, but in my mind, except for some lapses of memory, I don't feel old.

Neither am I looking back with a warm glow towards tradition. If I have learnt anything in the last years of my ministry it is that tradition can be a great hindrance to blessing. Tradition reveres activities and practices that worked well in the past, but the danger is to give to our traditions an authority that belongs only to Scripture. When we do that, it is impossible to change our activities and practices and replace them with something more appropriate to our present day.

Looking back can only be justified if we do so to praise the Lord for his past blessings and to learn from our past failures.

1.
THEN AND NOW

The world is a very different to place to when I was ordained in 1963. Then there were still certain standards of right and wrong. It was no more Christian than it is now, but at least there was a modicum of Christian influence over the public morality of the nation. Today much of this has gone – abortion, adultery, homosexuality and blasphemy are regarded as acceptable. Nothing is right or wrong any longer, everything is relative. It seems that today we can tolerate anything except a Biblical faith that insists on standards that are formulated by the Word of God. Today's society cannot stand this. They regard it as bigoted, intolerant and lacking in love.

Inevitably this has had a profound effect upon evangelical churches. We either retreat from the world and withdraw into our holy huddles, or we try and show the world that we are not really so different.

If we withdraw, we stop talking to unbelievers. We criticise, we sign petitions, but we do not evangelise. We forget how to talk to them in the language they can understand. We may still pay lip service to evangelism and every four or five years import into our church for a week or so an evangelist who we hope will do what we should have been doing every week. But the reality is that for us evangelism will have lost its urgency and relevance. When that happens we grow smaller and smaller and are soon struggling to keep the doors of the church open The Sunday school becomes a thing of the past, youth work all but disappears and our church becomes a gathering of old folk.

If we try to accommodate the world we have to lower our standards because there is no way that today's world will feel comfortable with Biblical standards. The gospel has never been seeker friendly; it never was in the New Testament and it will never be. To make it acceptable to an unregenerate person its teaching on sin and repentance has to be toned down.

Sadly this is what many evangelical churches have done. It is popular but it is not Biblical. It may get endless numbers of decisions for Christ, but are these genuine converts born again of the Holy Spirit with a new nature and a new lifestyle? The church's business is not to make the gospel acceptable to sinners but to make it understandable to them. There is a vital difference in this. To make it acceptable you have to tone it down. To make it understandable you tell it as it is in words that hearers can understand.

The question of lifestyle is crucial and Paul insists upon it in Ephesians 4:17, 'So I tell you this, and insist on it in

the Lord, that you must no longer live as the Gentiles do...'
Many evangelicals today would regard what the apostle
goes on to say in Ephesians 4 and 5 as legalism; but if we
cannot distinguish between legalism and obedience to the
Word of God then we are in serious trouble. Legalism is a
slavish adherence to a set of rules in order to obtain salvation. These rules can even be Biblical.

Dr. Kevan said, 'Legalism is an abuse of the law; it is
reliance on law-keeping for acceptance with God, and the
proud observance of laws is no part of the grace of God.'[1]
Obedience to Scripture is the fruit of a heart that loves the
Lord Jesus Christ. The obedience that Paul demands in
Ephesians 4 and 5 is impossible without the salvation he
has taught in Ephesians 2.

It is amazing how much sin can be excused by pleading
legalism. It is not unusual to hear Christians justifying their
sin by saying that God has not convicted them of a certain
behaviour. But does God have to convict when he has
already clearly commanded? A biblical command should
carry more weight with us than a subjective feeling.

☐ Behaviour

In the first 3 chapters of Ephesians Paul has been teaching
us the doctrines of the Christian faith, but doctrine is not
an end in itself. It is meant to be the basis and foundation
of our new life in Christ. What we believe will govern what
we do and Paul is saying that if we believe the doctrines
already taught then we ought to be living the sort of life he
sets before us in chapters 4-6.

Doctrine and practise are inseparable in New Testament Christianity. Whenever there is a decline of interest in doctrine there will inevitably, sooner or later, be a decline in Christian behaviour. The shallow evangelical life of today is a result of such a doctrinal decline. Some people think that you can have the Christian life without the doctrine, but that is impossible. We cannot change the New Testament order of things without paying a deadly price.

If the New Testament teaching is properly understood it will produce a life that honours and pleases God. By 'properly understood', we do not mean mere intellectual knowledge. It is possible to have all the right answers to questions but for those truths never to have moved from the head to the heart. When this happens you get a cold, formal, loveless, proud orthodoxy that is as far removed from New Testament Christianity as are liberal theology and humanism. The right answers do not prove that doctrines are properly understood. We need right answers plus a right life.

If we water down our teaching on salvation then inevitably we will have to water down our teaching on Christian behaviour. If we abandon the doctrine of justification then we will not need a doctrine of sanctification because sanctification is impossible without justification. To ask a person who has only accepted Christ as his Saviour but has never himself been accepted by Christ – which is the biblical doctrine of salvation and the way salvation is described in the scriptures – to live a sanctified life is futile. They cannot do it.

The problem is magnified when our watered down teaching becomes the standard for Christians who have been genuinely saved. So our standards of behaviour in the church have changed dramatically. We accept things today that would have been anathema forty years ago. For instance, our attitude towards the Lord's Day may be drastically different. It could be justifiably argued that some of things we used to do, or not do, on Sundays were governed more by tradition than Scripture, but is our present use of Sunday more biblical now than it used to be? Is it more beneficial to the health of our souls? Are we the better for our more liberal attitude?

Consider then the morality of today's evangelicals. I can remember in my college days a student who was liberal in his theology, saying that you never hear of evangelicals leaving the ministry or committing adultery. He may have been right forty years ago, but sadly this is not so today. Why is this? Doctrinal problems usually precede moral problems. If the biblical doctrines do not take hold of us, excite us, motivate us, and thus govern our lives, then even though we pay lip service to them we will have no more than what A. W. Tozer called a 'pseudo faith'.

Listen to Tozer, 'To many Christians Christ is little more than an idea or at best an ideal; he is not a fact. Millions of professed believers talk as if he were real and act as if he were not. And always our actual position is to be discovered by the way we act, not by the way we talk. We can prove our faith by our committal to it, and in no other way. Any idea that does not command the one who holds it is not a real belief; it is a pseudo belief only.'[2]

□ Suspicion

All the confusion in present day evangelicalism has led to an acute defence mechanism kicking in for some who see the problems but have no ideas on how to solve them. This has led to a suspicion of Christians who do not do everything exactly as we do. I don't doubt that to some extent this has always been a problem in the church, but never as pronounced as it is now.

Church growth and conversions are so rare today that when we hear of some church experiencing this blessing we can so easily become suspicious. We conclude that they must be compromising somewhere. Suspicion leads to wrong conclusions given to explain away their success.

What the wrong conclusions are will depend upon our particular viewpoint. For instance, in the mid-1970's the church of which I was pastor in Rugby, in the UK, were experiencing remarkable growth and regular conversions. Immediately a rumour started in South Wales (my home area) that Peter Jeffery had gone charismatic, while in Leicester it was being said that there was a large notice in the porch in Rugby stating that, 'the speaking in tongues is forbidden in this church.' Neither rumour was correct. The truth was that God was blessing a church that was reformed in doctrine and not charismatic, but neither was it cold, dry and lifeless.

Why do we find it so difficult to accept that God can bless those with whom we do not always agree? It may surprise some Calvinists to discover that some Charismatics have a deep and genuine love for the Lord. And it may

shock some Arminians to discover that some Calvinists have
a real evangelistic concern to reach out into their commu-
nities with the gospel. Even the way we describe each other
reveals this dismissive attitude – *wild* charismatic, *rank*
Arminians, *cold* Calvinists.

Suspicion breeds fear – and fear can have no place in a
local church. We get so fearful of some new idea coming
into our church that we may become irrational in our
defence of the traditional ways. I was preaching one
Sunday at a church I knew very well and was aware of
difficulties between those who wanted a traditional pattern
of worship and those who were more contemporary
minded. About 4pm I received a phone call from a friend
who was a member of this church. He wanted to know
who was leading the evening service. He knew I was preaching but was concerned who was leading. I knew what was
in his mind. He was afraid that one of the deacons, who
favoured a contemporary style of worship, would be leading, and if that were the case he would not attend. He was
right in his assumption, this deacon was to lead and consequently my friend went some where else.

This greatly troubled me and I went to the service that
night very curious to see what this particular contemporary style of worship was that so upset some Christians. It
certainly was not the hymn sandwich but it was dignified,
not noisy, reverent and greatly helped in preparing me to
preach to the church.

It is easy to become so afraid of what we call 'the thin
edge of the wedge', that everything new is resisted tena-
ciously. This can affect even the points in the service where

we give the announcements and how we take up the offer-
ing. It is true that such thinking has its reasons. There have
been cases where a small pressure group in a church has
forced its views on the majority, undermined the authority
of the Pastor and split the church. So the fear is not always
unjustified, but even then a church governed by fear and
suspicion is on very precarious ground.

2.
WORSHIP

When the charismatic movement irrupted upon the evangelical churches in the 1960s, its teaching on the miraculous, healing and tongues was not altogether new. The Pentecostal churches had been majoring in these for many years. The difference was that now the teaching had entered Anglican, Baptist, Brethren and all kinds of churches that were not Pentecostal. Inevitably it caused trouble. Some embraced it wholeheartedly while others in the same church opposed it just as wholeheartedly. There were splits and new churches were formed that were totally charismatic.

But even in churches where spiritual gifts were not a problem, the new style of worship brought in by the Charismatics was. This is still the case 40 years on and worship is the most contentious issue in many of today's evangelical churches.

Before the 1960's evangelicals tended to belong doctrinally to one of two camps – those who were Calvinistic or Reformed, and those who were Arminians. But basically their styles of worship were the same. Some sung choruses but this was not the real issue and usually Arminian and Calvinist could worship together with little or no trouble. Today, evangelicals are still divided doctrinally but there is also another division, namely their attitude to contemporary worship. It is this that causes serious problems because it prevents believers worshipping together,

Those who like contemporary Christian worship speak disparagingly about the old hymn sandwich, and those who love the old traditional ways will not tolerate new songs and new instruments. There seems to be no middle ground. Some churches try to accommodate both, even going to the extreme of having two different worship services in different parts of the building at the same time, and then all coming together for the sermon. But there is no way this accommodation will last for very long.

Other churches use both traditional and new hymns and this appears to be acceptable in many local situations. But even then there are problems. Those with traditional views may look suspiciously at such an arrangement. They may not go so far as to call the churches that use both 'charismatic', but the suspicion is there. And some Christians in these churches stand with lips firmly closed when a new hymn is sung.

□ Hymns

What we call today a traditional style of worship was not always traditional. Once it was very new and had to face the same opposition new hymns and songs face today. For centuries our churches sang only Psalms and many did so with no musical instrument at all. John Calvin regarded the organ as the Pope's instrument.

As early as the 17th Century there was a split in John Bunyan's church over the matter of singing. This was not resolved until after Bunyan's death, 'when it was decided that those who were conscientiously opposed to song could either remain silent or wait in the vestibule until the singing was over.'[1]

S. M. Houghton writes, 'From the Reformation until the 18th Century it was the custom to sing Psalms translated metrically by Sternhold and Hopkins. This belonged to the Puritan tradition and derived from John Calvin. The Sternhold and Hopkins' version was bound up in the same covers as the Bibles in private use, so that many regarded them as virtually on a level with Holy Writ. So their use tended to die hard. But Isaac Watts insisted that in confining songs of praise to the Book of Psalms, the worshipper was behaving as if Christ had never been born, had never died, and had never been raised from the dead and "received up into glory". He argued that in his day Christian praise lacked a New Testament content and he did his utmost to supply this lack. "To him, more than to any other man, is due the triumph of the hymn in Christian worship," says a modern scholar. Gradually the arguments of Watts prevailed. The Methodist Movement assisted the change, for in the person of Charles Wesley hymnody found its second greatest contributor. Once the fashion became established, many other men and several women contributed verses. In 1779 there appeared the *Olney Hymns* written by John Newton and William Cowper. The first Methodist *Psalms and Hymns* appeared as early as 1737, when John Wesley, its compiler, was a "Missioner in Georgia". He published a far more substantial hymnbook in the same year as the *Olney Hymns* appeared. The exclusive use of the metrical Psalms died hard, indeed, it is still retained in certain Scottish Churches, but gradually most Protestant churches welcomed the innovation and most modern hymn-books now contain a wealth of hymns, original and in translation, from many lands and centuries.'[2]

The battles of the 17th and 18th centuries are being fought again today. Then it was Psalms against hymns, now it is traditional hymns against more modern ones. To be fair some would object and say it is good hymns against poor ones. They argue that the modern songs are poor in content and sometimes trite. They also say that they are too subjective and do not dwell enough on the glory and majesty of God. There is truth in this concerning some of the new songs, but to generalise can be misleading. A Christian once described all modern songs to me as being rubbish. He could never have read the words of, '*As the deer pants for the water*', or '*There is a Redeemer*', or '*The price is paid.*' How can such words be called rubbish?

It is also objected that the modern songs will not stand the test of time as the old ones have. But when has that ever been different? Charles Wesley wrote over 6,000 hymns, but how many do we sing today?

Advocates of contemporary worship argue that we need modern music and hymns in our services so that unbelievers relate to them. It is good to bear in mind the unbeliever's reaction to our services. If they are confronted with mediocre music and pathetic singing then it is not surprising when they do not come back. But if we think that music alone is enough to attract unbelievers, we are living in cuckoo land. The world will always provide music that is more suited to their taste – but having said that, music is not unimportant.

The danger for the traditionalists is to almost sanctify the organ and piano and to see all other instruments as of the devil. If the music gets in the way of the words then it is a very serious issue. Gospel truth is expressed through words not musical notes. But surely we want the best music to help convey such a glorious message.

The same is true about archaic words and phrases that we find in some old hymns. Believers, let alone unbelievers, have difficulty in understanding 'the wormwood and the gall'. A retired businessman began to attend church. His wife was a Christian but he was not. He was a lovely man – kind, courteous, polite and not contentious. One day he said to me that he usually stopped singing the hymns after about two verses because he could not understand what he was singing about. How was I to respond to that? Should I dismiss it as a negative criticism? Should I think that because he is an unbeliever he would not be able to understand? Or should I take it seriously? If he had said that about the sermon I would have had to look seriously at my preaching – its presentation and language. So if it is possible to make our sermons understandable to unbelievers, is it not possible to make our hymns understandable to them also?

It may be objected that hymns in worship are not addressed to believers or unbelievers but to Almighty God. That is true but they have to be expressed in such a way as to be understandable to the worshipper or there can be no worship in the singing.

Listen to John Frame, 'Because God is who he is, worship must be God-centred. We worship God because he supremely deserves it, and because he desires it. We go to worship to please him, not ourselves. In that sense, worship is *vertical*, focused on God. We should not go to worship to be entertained, or to increase our self-esteem, but to honour our Lord who made and redeemed us.

'This is not to deny, however, that worship brings benefits to the worshipers. The benefits to the church can be summarised in terms like "edification", "strengthening"· and "upbuilding" (see 1 Corinthians 14:26 in different translations). There are also benefits to unbelieving visitors: conviction of sin and an encounter with the presence of God (1 Corinthians 14:24-25). In these ways, worship has a *horizontal*, as well as a vertical dimension.

'There is no contradiction between the vertical and the horizontal, between the God-centredness of worship and the benefits available to the worshipers. For it is that very God-centredness that blesses us. Meditating on God's greatness and his saving work in Christ is what enables us to grow in our devotion and obedience and thus to experience more and more the blessing of God in our lives. The horizontal dimension of worship, therefore, does not open the door wide to anything that happens to please the worshippers.'[3]

The great danger from music, whether it be traditional or contemporary, is that is that it can be allowed to dominate worship and relegate preaching to a secondary role. This was a danger before the days of modern hymns and happened, for instance, in the 1904-05 revival in Wales. It is a serious danger today and should be avoided at all costs.

It is awareness of the God-centredness of worship that will stop it from degenerating into noisy entertainment. Worship can and should be dignified and reverent but still be contemporary.

3.
Bible versions

If you were a Christian in 1960 you almost certainly would have used the Authorised Version of the Bible. There were a few alternatives but none were a serious option for most evangelicals. By 1990 all this had changed and in that year both the Good News Bible and the New International Version were outselling the AV in the bookshops.

At that time, in most congregations, you would probably have found four or five different versions being used. This often caused confusion, particularly for the young convert. I remember preaching on the text in Matthew 17:21 – 'Howbeit this kind goeth not out but by prayer and fasting' (AV). In the congregation was a young man who had only been converted few weeks, and I could see when I gave out the text that he looked very puzzled. I discovered afterwards what his problem was: he was using a RSV Bible, and in that version Matthew 17:21 is omitted. So my text was not in his Bible!

□ Translation or paraphrase?

Another more serious source of confusion is the use of a paraphrase version. A paraphrase attempts to 'take the original thought and convert it into the language of today' (K. M. Taylor) – or, to quote *The Concise Oxford Dictionary,* a paraphrase is a 'free rendering or amplification of a passage'. On the surface this sounds very helpful, but it does give rise to serious problems of accuracy.

For example, the AV, RSV and NIV are translations; but the *Living Bible,* of which many million copies have been sold since 1971, is a paraphrase. What is the difference between a translation and a paraphrase? Well, the translator looks at the original Hebrew and Greek and asks the question, 'What does it *say*?' while the translator who is producing a paraphrase looks at the original languages and asks the question, 'What does it *mean*?' You may think there is not much difference between these two questions, but there is, and they can produce different answers. The danger of a paraphrase is that it does not always translate the original accurately. Inevitably, 'What does it mean?' becomes 'What do I think it means?' – and so words and thoughts are added that are not in the original. The *Living Bible* is guilty of this in many places.

A glaring example of this is John 1:17. The AV reads, 'For the law was given by Moses, but grace and truth came by Jesus Christ.' The *Living Bible* reads, 'Moses gave us only the Law with its rigid demands and merciless justice, while Jesus Christ brought us loving forgiveness as well.' In this version much is added which is not biblically true.

Moses did not give us *only* the law, for Jesus said, 'he wrote about me'. The law in the Old Testament was certainly not merciless, but speaks of the mercy of God in many places. You will notice also that the *Living Bible* leaves out the reference to Jesus bringing *truth*.

Paraphrases may be easier to read and understand, but this in no way makes up for the inaccuracies. Such versions can be helpful, but they should only be used along-side a good translation.

☐ What is a good translation?

A clue to the issue of accuracy may be given in the attitude of the translators themselves to Scripture. Do they believe in the authority and inspiration of the Word of God? Do they agree with the teaching and doctrines of the Bible? This is no small point. For example, the translators of many modern versions do not believe in the wrath of God. The Bible is very clear on this doctrine, but many translators reject it. Consequently, when they have to deal with a word like 'propitiation' (Romans 3:25 AV), which means Christ turning away the wrath of God from the sinner by his substitutionary death on the cross, they change the word to 'expiation' (RSV and New English Bible), which means Christ taking away our sins.

It is true that Christ is an expiation for us; he did take away our sin; but that is not what Paul is saying in Romans 3:25. Here is a case where the translation of the word is affected by the doctrinal beliefs of the translators. As Dr Lloyd-Jones puts it, 'It is an example of a translation that has already become exposition. It has put a word which has a different meaning in place of the word used by the Apostle.' Of the many modern versions, some at least have been translated by men who are faithful to the authority and meaning of Scripture, such as the NASB, NKJV and NIV.

Basically what the Christian requires is a translation that is accurate and understandable. Many young Christians find the AV difficult to understand for, apart from the use of 'thee' and 'thou', many words have changed their meaning since the seventeenth century. It is not difficult to determine what you can understand and what you cannot, but not many believers are in a position to decide which version is accurate and which is not. Here you need guidance and advice, and you would be well advised to speak to your pastor about this matter.

□ The AV debate

For many believers the AV is their favoured version and they are not inclined to use any other. This is understandable and the choice is theirs. The problem arises when some then go a step further and dismiss all other versions as perversions. During the 1980s and 1990s there was a great debate as to the worth of versions, particularly the NIV, which was by then very popular with evangelicals. This debate grew rather hot when churches discussed whether or not to use the NIV along side the AV for public worship. Some Christians even left their churches when the NIV was introduced.

The AV was deeply loved and for very good reasons. Its language is beautiful and it has occupied a large place in the hearts and minds of generations of Christians. These believers saw no need for a new translation and were suspicious of anything that threatened to replace the AV. But the AV itself has seen several revisions. It was translated in 1611 but that version only lasted for 18 years and was revised in 1629, and then again in 1638. In 1762 a third revision was undertaken, the aim being to restore the Bible to current literary English. A fourth revision took place in 1769 and this is what we have today as the Authorised Version or as the Americans call it, the King James Version.

The AV is as accurate as any version but no translation is without its faults. Caution is needed when assessing one version against another. It is possible to have double standards and refuse to apply the same criticism to the AV as to the NIV. The AV has its problems of accuracy as Dr. Lloyd-Jones points out several times in his exposition of Romans 5. For example, on verse 12 he writes, 'The first thing to determine is the correct translation; and unfortunately, the Authorised Version is not good here.' He makes similar comments on other verses. Lloyd-Jones was unquestionably an AV man, but clearly he was not averse to using other translations in his exposition of Romans.

The NIV is not without its problems but its strength is that it is readable and understandable to the modern man. This is the version used by most evangelicals today though in recent years the New King James Version has also become popular.

4.
The Ministry

For about ten years, from the mid-1950s-60s, the Lord called an unusual number of young men into the ministry. From my hometown of Neath there were eleven of us. All but one of these trained in denominational colleges and then took their first pastorates in denominational churches that contained very few born again believers. It was a difficult time but it was also a time of expectancy. Did God have some great blessing in preparation? Surely he had not called all these men to preach for no reason. My first church was in Monmouthshire and there I attended an evangelical minister's fellowship of forty members. Ten years before there would hardly have been a handful of evangelicals in the whole county.

Most of these men were very good preachers but now at the beginning of the 21st century they are all retired or close to retirement, and the land is spiritually more barren than it was then. Their ministry was faithful and often powerful. There were conversions but not enough to make any difference to society. The great blessing we so eagerly expected never materialised, and now a new generation of pastors has to take on the work.

I do not envy these men because the work is harder now than it was in 1960. The churches are smaller so there are fewer workers, and also less money to finance the ministry. I dread to think what stipend some of these pastors receive in the small churches. I admire these young men but I have also some concerns about them. There are a few excellent preachers among them but most seem to lack fire in their bones. They lecture well but lack the ability to preach and herald out the gospel.

□ Preaching

A few years ago I visited California and was introduced to a church as 'Peter Jeffery who had come from Britain to share the gospel with them'. I replied, politely, that I had not come 6,000 miles to share anything with them. I had come to preach, to tell them what the Word of God says. 'Sharing' is too insipid a word to describe preaching. Preaching is heralding, proclaiming, and telling out the good news of the Lord Jesus Christ. It ought to have a measure of authority about it and not leave people with a 'take it or leave it' choice. It should confront men and women with God and eternity. Preaching the gospel declares that the one and only way to God is through Jesus; therefore it should never be boring. It is always relevant and always urgent.

How then can evangelical preachers be boring? Why do we leave our congregations cold and unmoved? During the winter of 1981-82 I was unable to preach for seven months before and after a heart by-pass operation. I could attend church only for the morning services and with a few exceptions I was shocked at what I was hearing. Students from theological college seemed to be delivering the lectures they had heard during the week, and they were taking an hour to do so. What they were saying was true and biblical but it was dry, lifeless and boring. I determined there and then that when I was able to preach again I would not preach so that people were longing for me to finish.

How I succeeded in this others will have to decide, but I certainly give more thought to my hearers now than I use to. Some young preachers seem to forget that they are not in the pulpit for their sakes but for the glory of God and the spiritual well being of the people who are listening to them. If they thought more about the people they would not preach so long. For young men to preach for over an hour is, I believe, arrogance. There are few experienced men, let alone students, who can hold the attention of their hearers profitably for over an hour.

This is not the grousing of an old man but the deep concern of a man who loves preaching too much to see it deteriorate into lecturing. There is a place for lecturing, but not in the pulpit on a Sunday. Our people need their hearts warmed as well as their heads filled.

There appears today a distinct reluctance with some evangelicals to preach the gospel. They seem to have no problem teaching the faithful the disciplines of the Christian life but seem unable to preach to lost souls in a direct and understandable way. Some don't even see a need to do so. They argue that almost all our congregations consist of believers so why preach to unbelievers if they are not there? But they seem to miss the point that our folk will never invite sinners; friends, neighbours and relatives to church, if they know they will not hear the gospel when they come. And is it not true that there is nothing more thrilling for a Christian to hear than the message of the cross.

□ Preaching the Gospel

The gospel preacher must have a passion for the souls of men and women. He is not preaching to teach them but to see them saved. Every gospel sermon should have this glorious aim. He must also love the people. Richard Cecil said, 'To love to preach is one thing; to love those to whom we preach is quite another. If you lack this element of compassion for the people, you will also lack the pathos which is a very vital element of true preaching.'

It is this love and pathos that brings into gospel preaching what Dr. Lloyd-Jones called a 'melting quality'. What a phrase that is! It is possible to be too harsh in our gospel preaching, delighting to tell sinners they are going to hell. We must preach this, but, oh, to be able to do so with this melting quality.

The gospel preacher must preach to where the people are not where he would like them to be. Today most people are biblically illiterate so one must preach to that condition. This means simply, clearly and free of jargon.

George Whitefield said, 'I use market language.' Spurgeon said, 'The multitudes will never be benefited by preaching which requires them to bring a dictionary to church.' Plain speech is not slang but language and concepts that people can understand and illustrations they can relate to.

• The task of the evangelist

On spiritual matters we are to address men and women who are spiritually dead, that is, people who are incapable of understanding spiritual truths because the devil has blinded their minds. We are just like Ezekiel before the valley of dry bones. Written right across the situation is the word 'impossible'. Spurgeon said, 'No minister living can save a soul; nor can all of us together, nor all the saints in heaven or in earth. We cannot work the regeneration of a single person. The whole business on our part is the height of absurdity.'

Then why even try? There are two reasons …

♦ We ourselves were once spiritually dead and the impossible happened to us. We were saved.

♦ The impossible is possible only because of God. It is God alone who saves, but He has chosen to use the means of preaching to accomplish salvation, and, therefore, preaching the gospel is crucial.

All this requires that the gospel preacher have an unwavering trust in God and an unshakeable confidence in the message he is preaching. It is this alone that keeps us going. If our confidence is in anything else, sooner or later it will let us down, and we will become demoralised and disillusioned.

- **The task of the gospel preacher is the salvation of souls, and he should be satisfied with nothing less.**

We must be faithful but even that is not enough. We must want success. The gospel is meant by God to save souls and, therefore, it ought to save. I wonder if we think the word 'success' is unspiritual? Richard Baxter said, 'If you would prosper in your work be sure to keep up earnest desires and expectations of success. God seldom blesses any man's work so much as his whose heart is set on success. Let all that preach Christ and man's salvation be unsatisfied until they have the things they preach for.'

- **The task of the preacher is to reach the heart of the sinner.**

Spurgeon said, 'A sinner has a heart as well as a head; a sinner has emotions as well as thoughts, and we must appeal to both. A sinner will never be converted until his emotions are stirred.'

For most preachers the easy part is to preach the truth, to give a faithful exposition of Scripture. The difficult thing is to preach in such a way that we stir the hearts and prick the consciences of sinners. An easy way out is to say that only the Holy Spirit can do that. But is this a correct attitude for it so often causes us to give up our responsibilities as preachers and reduce preaching to mere lecturing?

- **How do we preach so that sinner's hearts and emotions are stirred?**

It is not by filling the sermon with sentimental stories of dying children. This may well stir the emotions, but it will not lead to salvation. It is the action of the actor, not the preacher. Neither is it by packing the service with gimmicks and working up an atmosphere. So what is the answer?

By preaching to them and for them. This means we must have plenty of application all the way through the sermon – pointing out truths, pushing them home and showing their relevance to every day affairs of life. In this way we will guard against being heavy and boring.

What a privilege the gospel preacher has to stand before people who are dead in sin and tell them that God loves them. Then to prove it by telling them of Jesus, the glories of the incarnation, Calvary, prophecies fulfilled, divine justice satisfied, and the resurrection; to tell them that God demands the response of repentance and faith!

What a privilege to preach the gospel! What a joy to see the Holy Spirit begin to work in sinners – indifference turning to concern, concern to conviction, conviction to salvation!

☐ The Church and its pastor

Paul preached at Ephesus for three years and in spite of much opposition his ministry was greatly blessed by God. It was very difficult therefore for him to leave. His final meeting with the Ephesian elders was an emotional one (Acts 20: 36-37). These men loved Paul and so it should always be with a pastor and his people. Pastors are not to be put on a pedestal but they are to be loved, valued and respected on account of the truths of God, which they teach the people. A church, which has a preacher who loves the Lord and loves them, is highly favoured. A man who can preach the word in a powerful and enlightening way is to be valued.

No pastor is perfect and they all make mistakes but if their preaching both warms the heart and instructs the mind, there should be the same sort of feeling towards them as the Ephesians showed to Paul. Most pastors get more than their fair share of criticisms, some deserved some not, but they should also get the support and prayers of their church. A pastor that is loved and prayed for will be a better preacher. There is no doubt that a church can make or break a preacher.

- **If your pastor is not as good as you think he ought to be, try praying more earnestly for him.**

√ Pray for unction and power on his preaching.
√ Pray for love and wisdom on his pastoral work.
√ Pray that his life will be enriched daily by the presence of the Lord.
√ Pray that next Sunday when he enters the pulpit he will have a message from the Lord for you and the church.

- **Don't wait until he leaves the church to weep, but do so now in passionate prayer for his work.**

5.
Elders and Deacons

In the 1970s evangelical churches looked seriously at the question of eldership. Prior to this most of the churches, apart from those with a Presbyterian background, did not have elders. The Baptist and Congregational church pattern was to have deacons only. It was often argued that the deacons did the work of elders and this was deemed to be all that was necessary. How biblical such thinking was is open to doubt. If the New Testament recognises both elders and deacons as part of God's plan for his church, why should we only have deacons?

Evangelical churches began to grapple with the subject of elders and some got very excited about it. They saw eldership as solving most of their problems, but it did not. As some churches discovered, it is better to have no elders than the wrong elders. It may be a rather obvious thing to say, but if a local church does not have men who are biblically qualified for eldership then it cannot have elders. To fill the office for the sake of it is a sure way to trouble.

Having said that, it is God's will that his church should have structure and this includes the leadership of elders and deacons. This is because men and women need leadership. Without it things would not be done decently and in order because, as sinners, we are more prone to chaos than order. Examples of this abound in the New Testament.

There is the chaos of wrong doctrine (1 Tim. 1:3-7). Who is to deal with this? Paul tells Timothy that it is his responsibility as the pastor/elder of the church. It is a spiritual problem and those men called elders are charged to deal with it (1 Tim. 3:4-5).

There is the chaos of bad management, which we see in Acts 6. Who is to deal with this? The apostles could have tackled this problem themselves, but that would have meant neglecting their prime ministry of prayer and preaching. So men that we normally recognise as deacons were chosen to deal with it and they did so with sensitivity and skill.

All chaos, whether spiritual or material, will hinder the progress of the gospel, so God decrees that men with certain spiritual qualities and gifts be appointed so that such problems may be avoided, or if not avoided, then dealt with swiftly when they arise.

□ Difficulties of leadership

No leader of God's people has ever had an easy task. Paul tells Timothy that he is to '...command certain men not to teach false doctrines' (1 Tim. 1:3). The same word, 'command', is also used in 1 Timothy 4:11 and 6:17-18. But people do not like being commanded, especially when they

are wrong, and so the one doing the commanding can
expect criticism. Because of this, certain qualities are
essential for leaders. The elder must not be violent or quar-
relsome but gentle (1 Tim. 3:3). This is necessary because
if elders were to react in the same way as they are sometimes treated, there would be civil war in the church.
Deacons must be men worthy of respect (1 Tim. 3:8). This
respect will have been earned over a period of time and
Christians will have learnt to trust them and value their
opinions. This will be of immense value in defusing difficult situations.

• Pastor and elder

The New Testament has much to say about elders though
it does not always call them by this name. Sometimes they
are also called 'bishops' or 'overseers'. This is clearly seen
in Titus 1:5-7, where the words 'elder' and 'overseer' are
used to describe the same function. 'Bishop' means the
same as 'overseer' and, unlike today, when one bishop has
responsibility for several churches, in the New Testament
one church had several bishops/overseers/elders. So we
read in Acts 20:17 of the elders (plural) at the church in
Ephesus.

In 1 Timothy 5:17 Paul seems to suggest that there are
two types of elders: those who direct the affairs of the church,
and those whose work is preaching and teaching. These
are normally known as ruling elders and preaching elders,
or more usually in our churches today as elders and
pastors. All elders direct the affairs of the church but some

have a particular responsibility for preaching. They specialise in this, work hard at it, give time and study to prepare for preaching and as such they are paid by the church (1 Tim. 5:17-18).

The pastor is a teaching elder – his prime responsibility is the ministry of the Word – but all elders share to a degree in this responsibility because all should be able to teach (1 Tim. 3:2). This does not mean that every elder should be able to preach, but because his ministry is spiritual, he must be able to direct and counsel Christians in a personal one-to-one ministry. Therefore in the words of Titus 1:9: 'He must hold firmly to the trustworthy message as it has been taught, so that he can encourage others by sound doctrine and refute those who oppose it.'

Paul has several things to say to Timothy as a pastor and preacher that are applicable to all pastors and preachers. The pastor is a man with a special gift (1 Tim. 4:14). This will include the natural abilities of speech and intelligence, but it is far more than that, as the verse makes clear.

He has been given a special gift from God, bestowed upon him by the Holy Spirit and recognised by the church. It is this alone that qualifies him for ministry. The gift must be carefully guarded and not neglected. This is done by the pastor's own spiritual relationship with God and the truths of God: 'Be diligent in these matters; give yourself wholly to them, so that everyone may see your progress. Watch your life and doctrine closely. Persevere in them, because if you do, you will save both yourself and your hearers.'

Furthermore, a good minister will preach the truth to the church, even though at times it is not popular (1 Tim. 4:6) and he will not be side-tracked by irrelevancies (1 Tim. 4:7).

The elder is to rule. The function of leadership is to lead and not to wait for a consensus of opinion. But this leadership is not to be domineering; rather it is the leadership of the shepherd whose prime concern is for the well being of the flock (1 Peter 5:2-3). He leads by the personal example of his life shown in his enthusiasm and diligence for the work of the gospel and for the church (Titus 1:7-8).

☐ How should the church behave towards these men?

We should see them as appointed by God (Acts 20:28) and as such we should honour them (1 Tim. 5:17) and treat them with respect because of their office. They are not above criticism but the church must be careful as to how it deals with accusations against an elder (1 Tim. 5:19). The reputation of an elder must not be unnecessarily damaged and his work hindered. None the less, if an elder is guilty of sin it is such a serious matter that he must be publicly rebuked (1 Tim. 5:20).

• Deacons

The qualifications required for a deacon in 1 Timothy 3 are very similar to those for elders. This is because the difference between the two offices is functional, not one of character. It is not that the elders are more spiritual men than deacons, but that their gifts and calling are different.

□ Tensions

A church with good elders and deacons is greatly favoured. Men operating biblically in these offices should be able to deal with all the problems and tensions that arise in a local church. Though, it has to be said, there are sometimes tensions between elders and deacons. Some elders are not prepared for deacons to exercise any authority. They want the control of the finances of the church as well as operating a pastoral oversight. They see the deacon as a sort of assistant instead of an office in its own right. This causes deacons to resent the elders and many a church has known this tension.

Some deacons desire to be 'promoted' to the eldership and regard their work as deacons as inferior. They may feel that they ought to be elders not deacons. Such a spirit disqualifies a man from any office in the church.

But the worst problem are elders who are only committee-men. They love to meet once a month to decide church policy but do not take any pastoral responsibility. They are elders in name but not in reality. This is recognised very often by the church and then all respect for the eldership is lost. In some churches there is no mechanism for removing elders from office and resentment and tensions then grow apace.

All this makes it necessary for churches to be very careful who they appoint as elders and deacons. The biblical requirements spelt out in 1 Timothy should be taken seriously. It is better to have only one or two men in office who meet this standard than twelve who do not.

6.
Moaners and groaners

Moaners and groaners are not new in the church, even Moses in the Old Testament had his problems with them – '...The whole community grumbled against Moses and Aaron.' (Exodus 16:2). Nearly always their grumbling was against the blessings of the Lord. They probably never saw it like that, but to argue '...It would have been better for us to serve the Egyptians than to die in the desert' (Exodus 14:12), was to despise the redemptive grace of God in bringing them out of slavery. In the New Testament Paul's life was plagued with the groans of those who professed salvation.

Why is it that Christians are so prone to moaning? Are we so super sensitive that we cannot take the difficulties and knocks of the Christian life? Or perhaps it is that many Christians have never understood the true nature of the spiritual battle we are in. 'Come to Jesus, and all your problems will be over' is the message we hear from some preachers. Certain hymns and choruses also seem to confirm this teaching. Unfortunately, however, this is not the Christian's experience after conversion and, more importantly, not what the Scriptures teach.

When a person comes to Christ in repentance and faith, sin, his greatest problem, is dealt with. The joy of salvation and the experience of peace with God can be overwhelming, and with some this may last for days, weeks or even months. But eventually other problems, completely unknown in pre-conversion days, will begin to make themselves felt. As a result, far from being full of joy and happiness the young Christian will know the misery of doubts, guilt and conviction of sin as never before. On top of all this, he will have to face misunderstanding and opposition to his newfound faith from both friends and relatives.

All this can seem quite devastating to the new convert, but the Scriptures assure us that it is only to be expected. The Lord Jesus Himself said to His disciples, '...In the world you will have trouble...' (John 16:33). And the apostle Paul, returning to strengthen and encourage churches he had established on his first missionary journey, told them, '...We must go through many hardships to enter the kingdom of God...' (Acts 14:22).

Why should it be like this? The fact is that when we become Christians, we do not enter not a holiday camp where everything is jolly and comfortable, but rather a battle station in the middle of a fierce war. We are now soldiers in the Lord's army, and the enemy exerts tremendous pressure upon us.

☐ Moaners and groaners are usually ...

• Shortsighted

They forget past blessings and are absorbed in present difficulties. In such a condition it is not unusual to hear Christians speak enviously of unbelievers. They see non-Christians apparently devoid of the troubles they have to endure and begin to regret that they themselves are Christians. The Psalmist was beginning to go down this path – 'But as for me, my feet had almost slipped; I had nearly lost my foothold. For I envied the arrogant when I saw the prosperity of the wicked. They have no struggles; their bodies are healthy and strong. They are free from the burdens common to man; they are not plagued by human ills.' (Psalm 73:2-5). His conclusion was that it was a waste of time trusting in God – 'This is what the wicked are like – always carefree and increase in wealth. Surely in vain have I kept my heart pure; in vain have I washed my hands in innocence.' (verses 12-13).

Why had the Psalmist sunk to such depths? Because he was evaluating things only on present experiences and had forgotten eternal truths. No wonder that when he tried to make sense of life's injustices that he was confused and oppressed. The remedy for him came when his vision lengthened, – 'When I tried to understand all this, it was oppressive to me 'till I entered the sanctuary of God; then I understood their final destiny.' A Christian is in a very sad state when he envies a man who is going to hell.

• Selfish

The groaner has little or no concern about how his actions effect other Christian. The person becomes so wrapped up in their problems, whether real or imaginary, that they care little of how their attitude depresses others. The Psalmist, for all his confused thinking, kept his thoughts to himself because, 'If I had said, I will speak thus, I would have betrayed your children.'

We all go through periods of bewilderment and bitterness but the remedy is not to pour it all out to any one who will listen. We may need some one to confide in but even then it ought to be a person who can cope with our groans, not some one who will finish up as depressed as we are. The moaner, by definition, just blurts it all out because he is concerned only with how he feels and has no thought for others.

• Spiritually blind

These are Christians who are unable to see and appreciate blessings from God. They complain that they preferred their church when it was small because then they knew everyone and despise the fact that God has blessed the church with growth. They are not prepared to take the trouble to get to know the newcomers and personal inconvenience blinds them into not seeing that they ought to be rejoicing in blessings.

A believer went to tell his pastor that he was taking his family to another church. The reason he gave was that he

had been in that church for six years and had only been
blessed in one service. That was a serious complaint. But
the pastor pointed out that those six years had seen
remarkable blessings from the Lord and over a hundred
souls had been saved in that period. So if souls were being
saved, why was he not being blessed? Was he so spiritually blind that he could not conceive that it might be him
and not the church, that was wrong?

☐ The remedy for groaners

We can find the remedy in two Old Testament passages.
The first of these is in Exodus 14 and tells us about the
Israelites at the Red Sea.

The difficulties these people faced were a direct consequence of who they were. They were God's people and
their problems were those of redemption. If they had not
been redeemed they would not have faced these particular problems. The difficulties were the Red Sea in front of
them and the Egyptians behind them. These were no phan-
tom problems but very real and serious – so much so that
the Israelites were terrified and saw no way out of their
predicament.

These people had recently been redeemed. All their lives
they had been in slavery with no hope of rescue. But God
had loved them and chosen them and exerted divine power
to set them free. They had sheltered under the blood of the
Passover Lamb and had been led in triumph from their
bondage. God had performed these incredible acts and
they knew it was the only way they could obtain redemption.

Slavery was behind them and they were on their way to the Promised Land.

What was true of them is also true of all Christians. We are redeemed from the bondage of sin. Our situation was hopeless but God loved us and chose us, and by exerting the divine power of grace, love and mercy, he saved us. The bondage of sin is behind us and heaven is before us. Of all people in this world none is as favoured and privileged as the Christian.

It was because of the blessing of redemption that the Israelites' difficulties arose. If they had not been redeemed they would never have been in the particular situation that terrified them. We need to appreciate that there are trials peculiar to the Christian and these are the direct result of coming out of the world. Far from being exempt from problems – as is sometimes suggested by the 'Come to Jesus and be happy' type of preaching – the Christian has to face all the difficulties that confront the non-Christian, such as health worries, family problems and financial concerns, plus a host of spiritual problems of which the unbeliever knows nothing. These are problems of redemption and of new life in Christ. They are part of the spiritual battle and Satan's opposition.

Take, for instance, guilt and conviction of sin. No one is saved without a sense of conviction of sin, but this does not end at conversion. For many Christians it is far stronger after they are saved than it was before. This is because our spirits are sensitive now to the intrusions of sin, and we feel deeply our failure and grieving of the Holy Spirit. Very often after the excitement of conversion we come down to earth with a bump as we realise that, though we are free from sin's slavery, its influence and temptation still bother us. Sometimes problems give rise to doubts and confusion. We cannot understand why God allows certain things to happen to us. We complain, and bitterness and resentment can soon flow from such complaints. This was the Israelites' attitude as they faced the Red Sea. It was blocking their way to the blessings of the Promised Land and they could not understand why they had to face this barrier.

Then there was the problem of the Egyptians behind them seeking to bring them back into slavery. This is a vivid picture of Satan and the world pursuing the Christian, and it is real to every believer, whether he or she has been converted only a short time, or for many years. Old desires which you thought were long buried suddenly flood back into your mind. Old feelings of resentment are inexplicably stirred up. The devil does not stop. He cannot rob you of your salvation, but he can disturb your assurance, peace and joy in the Lord.

These, and similar problems, are real and common, but the greatest difficulty we face as Christians is our own unbelief. This was the trouble with the Israelites; they were terrified and cried out to the Lord. They said to Moses, '...Was it because there were no graves in Egypt that you brought us to the desert to die? What have you done to us by bringing us out of Egypt? Didn't we say to you in Egypt, "Leave us alone; let us serve the Egyptians"? It would have been better for us to serve the Egyptians than to die in the desert!' (Exodus 14:10-12). They were forgetting the power of God which had already been demonstrated on their behalf in redemption. They were acting as if they had no God and everything depended upon them. Don't we often do the same? If we let it, fear will breed unbelief. Of course, it can also have the opposite effect and produce faith.

Moses expresses the remedy to this fear in his reply: 'Do not be afraid. Stand firm and you will see the deliverance the Lord will bring you today. The Egyptians you see today you will never see again. The Lord will fight for you; you need only to be still' (Exodus. 14:13–14). We need to remind ourselves of this truth frequently. When in grave difficulties, we need to remember the resources that are available to us as the redeemed children of God.

Difficulties depress us because we cannot cope with them and it seems as if there is no answer. We realise the limitations of our strength and ability when we are called upon to deal with serious problems. We are weak and many situations are beyond our capabilities. This may well be true, but it is of no consequence because, as Moses reminds us, 'The Lord will fight for you; you need only to be still.' Is this too simplistic, or is it the truth?

In Exodus 14 we read how God intervened and dealt with both the Red Sea and the Egyptians. Throughout Scripture he does the same thing; for example, with Joshua and the walls of Jericho, or Peter in prison. The same can be seen in church history. When Martin Luther made his famous stand against the abuses and heresies of the Roman Catholic Church, the pope dismissed it all as a monk's squabble. If it was only Luther being awkward the pope would have been right. But God was in it and the result was the mighty Reformation.

We can praise God that this principle is also true in our own lives. Stop for a moment and think of the times that God has met your needs. Maybe it was only in small things, but it was still from God. So you can trust him in every situation. The power of God working for his people is an awesome thing. No wonder Paul said, 'If God be for us, who can be against us?'

Now consider Asa in 2 Chronicles 14. Asa was one of the few good kings Israel or Judah had. Most were ungodly men who, by example and command, led the people away from God to worship idols. Asa was different, as is evident from 2 Chronicles 14:2-4. He '...did what was good and right in the eyes of the Lord his God. He removed the foreign altars and the high places, smashed the sacred stones and cut down the Asherah poles. He commanded Judah to seek the Lord, the God of their fathers, and to obey his laws and commands.'

As soon as he became king this man went into battle. It was a battle, not against the traditional enemies such as the Philistines or Midianites, but against the more powerful foes of sin and idolatry among the Lord's people. This was a real battle and it was one in which the Lord gave Asa the victory. The result was that for ten years there was peace with the other nations. God's people enjoyed a period of rest that was very unusual at that time, but it is an example of the biblical truth that righteousness exalts a nation.

When a nation, a church, or an individual, seeks to give the Lord his proper place in their lives, then the Lord honours this. Note in verse 6 that the peace they enjoyed was God-given and Asa understood this: '...we sought him and he has given us rest on every side...' (2 Chronicles. 14:7). The Bible says there is no peace for the wicked. This means that the person who submits to sin and lives outside the love and grace of God will never know rest and peace of soul. He is forever in bondage, a slave to sin. His will is not free and his eyes are blind to the good things of God. He may prosper in terms of material possessions but he has no real rest.

The Christian knows that rest is only found in Jesus. 'Come to me', the Saviour said, 'and I will give you rest.' But it is not the rest of indolence and laziness. We see in verse 7 that Asa used the rest to strengthen his defences. In the same way, the Christian realises that to maintain the God-given rest he must be forever diligent to keep down the influence of sin in his life. Jesus must be Lord and King, and reign supreme in the heart. This involves constant communion with Christ in prayer and Bible study, and regular oneness and fellowship with the people of God. In this way we strengthen our defences.

There is to be no peace treaty with sin. The Christian fights against it and that fight takes place primarily in the heart and mind. Strangely, in this fight, the peace and rest of God become more glorious and wondrous. This rest is not the rest of an armchair, neither is it a rest that makes the believer immune to outside pressures. Asa knew ten years of rest because the Lord gave it to him, but then in verse 9 we read that Zerah the Cushite came against him with a vast army. The Authorised Version tells us it was an army of a million men, one of the largest mentioned in Scripture.

Why did this happen? Was it that Asa had sinned and this was a punishment? There are no grounds in the context of the story to suggest this. Then why was this godly man, and the people he had led back to God, suddenly called upon to face an enemy stronger than anyone else had faced before? Obviously the Lord allowed this and he did so not as a punishment but as an encouragement, that they might learn more of his love and care for them, and thus discover an even deeper rest and peace.

• Basic lessons

There is a tendency in most of us always to see difficulties as something terrible and not, as they sometimes are, as opportunities to discover new depths of God's love and provisions. There are basic spiritual lessons that we can never learn when things are going well. We need the problems and difficulties to teach us the meaning of really trusting in the Lord. They take our trust out of the realm of theory and into the hurly-burly of reality. There, all the impurities and deficiencies are burnt out, and we are left with nothing but to look to God. This may not be a pleasant experience, but it can be, and ought to be, a spiritually enriching one.

Asa had learnt from his dealings with the Lord that confidence in God was most reasonable. There is no one like God to help the powerless. Do we believe that? Then should we not have the same confidence? Such confidence creates simplicity in prayer. Asa does not waste time telling God all the details of the size of the armies. He just says,

'Lord they are mighty; we are powerless. Help us.' It was so simple. You don't need a degree in theology to pray like that. You don't need to have a silver tongue. The prayer was simple but powerful because the Lord loves to help his people in their needs.

The relationship of the Christian to their God is not a complex system of rituals, ceremonies and liturgies. It is simply a relationship of Father and child. So, 'help us', is both natural and appropriate.

7.
Where do we go from here?

There can be no doubt that the past 40 years have not been good ones for evangelical churches. Confusion, disputes and tensions within the church, as well as the growing godlessness of the world, have all worked to weaken the cause of the gospel. So where do we go from here?

The prime answer has to be that we need the Lord to do a work of revival in the churches – and we will look at that in a later chapter – but what can we do now to arrest the slide? Revival is a sovereign work of God and cannot be organised by man, but that does not mean there is nothing for us to do. The Scriptures will not allow us to sit back and wait for God to work. The Lord has placed very clear responsibilities upon his people and it is time that we faced up to these. In Ephesians 5:10 Paul urges us to '...find out what pleases the Lord', and the implication there is that having found out, we do it.

So what is it that pleases the Lord and what do we need to do so that we can '...Live as children of light.' (Ephesians 5:8).

□ We need a greater vision of God's greatness

A church cannot rise above its concept of God. If we have a small view of God then inevitably we will have no expectation of God breaking into our lives in power. No expectation produces dry formal lifeless Christianity that has a good memory for remembering past blessings but has no vision for present moves of God's Holy Spirit.

The prophet Haggai was called by God to minister to a people who were disillusioned and frustrated. Their hopes and expectations were shattered. The great days of the past, when they counted for something, were gone, and all that was left was a temple in ruins, problems on all sides and no real hope of ever accomplishing anything. Doesn't all this sound amazingly like our day? Gone are the big congregations and packed churches. We are in a post-Christian era. Like those in Haggai's time we are only a remnant but God has still given us a task. There is also another similarity that has to be noted. Their original zeal had gone. They had got caught up in their own pursuits and their God-given task was forgotten. How true this is of so many of today's people of God! Twenty years ago their zeal for the Lord's work knew no bounds. They gave unstintingly of their time and money, but not now. Other things, legitimate things, have taken priority and they have left the burden of God's work to others.

This was the situation that Haggai inherited. He did not create it but he had to deal with it. His message to the people is to think. Twice, in chapter 1, verses 5 and 7, he urges them to give careful thought to their situation. In verse 6, we have a vivid picture of a dissatisfied man, and this is not the man of the world, but a picture of a materially minded child of God whose priorities are all wrong.

Sadly this picture is too accurate for comfort in describing many of today's Christians. Dissatisfaction and disillusionment seem to characterize so many modern believers. They sing as if they are happy but they are not. They delight to proclaim, 'None but Christ can satisfy,' but they are not satisfied. Why is this so? What is the problem? These Christians will give all sorts of answers, but there is only one real issue here. The problem is the Christian's relationship with, and commitment to, the Lord. We seem to have lost our way, lost our expectations, lost our zeal and lost our first love. The answer is to think, to consider, to ponder on where we are spiritually. When we do that we shall see that there is only one way out of the dilemma – to turn back to God.

This is exactly the message of Haggai. What we need is a clearer vision of the greatness and glory of God, and a correspondingly greater commitment to him. Haggai proceeds to remind the people of basic truths about God.

• Start here

Haggai begins his ministry by reminding the people that their first priority must be to please God – '"This is what the Lord Almighty says; Give careful thought to your ways.

Go up into the mountains and bring down timber and build the house, so that I may take pleasure in it and be honoured," says the Lord.' (1:7-8). For Christians who are serious about God there is no other place to start. Is there something the Lord has been calling you to do that you have been delaying and excusing yourself from doing. Or perhaps you are guilty of just plain disobedience and stubbornly refuse to do it? Or it may be that you would like to do it but just feel so helpless. It seems way beyond your capabilities. Just remember the Lord often calls upon us to do what we cannot do. It is in this way that we learn to trust in his strength.

Haggai has some great encouragements for those who feel helpless – '...I am with you,' says the Lord, (1:13). Our God never leaves us to sink or swim. He always draws near to equip and strengthen, and this is the only guarantee of blessing. If God is with us it does not matter who is against us. This awareness transforms spiritual pigmies into giants and reduces mountains to molehills.

Perhaps Haggai's greatest encouragement is to remind us that nothing is impossible with God. Haggai 2:3 is a wonderful reminder that God's purposes are always fulfilled even though the situation may appear to be hopeless. The temple they were building would, according to the earlier prophets, surpass Solomon's temple in glory and splendour, but it all appeared totally improbable. The wise old heads who could remember the former glories probably dismissed the present work as a waste of time. Such pessimism is still with us, but God says, 'The glory of this present house will be greater than the glory of the former house...' (2:9). To lose sight of God, or doubt his purposes, means certain defeat, but to believe and hold on to these brings hope.

• God's power

The God of the Bible is a God of varied and limitless power and it is impossible to compare this with the greatest achievements of the mightiest men. Have you ever stood in a great cathedral and admired the huge structure and vast arches? You may wonder who made it. When you look in the guidebook you see it took thousands of men over a hundred years to construct that building. Then go outside and look at the sky, the stars and the moon; see the glory of the mountains and the sea, and ask, who made all this? The answer is that God did it alone and did it in a moment. He said, 'Let there be, ...' and there was. This is the power of God. I remember in the 1950s seeing the film *The Ten Commandments* and being particularly impressed with the scene of the opening of the Red Sea. I thought it was very clever, it looked so real. Then I suddenly thought, God actually did it. No trick camera work, but omnipotence parted those waters. That is real power.

A difficulty we have with divine omnipotence is that we misinterpret it. You do not have to read the Bible for very long to discover the difference in outlook between the men of Scripture and modern man. We are suffering from what Tozer called 'a secularised mentality'. Where those men saw God, we see the laws of nature. We have reduced the omnipotent God to a set of laws and forget that what we see in nature is simply the paths that God's power and wisdom take. As Tozer put it, 'Science observes how the power of God operates, discovers a regular pattern somewhere and fixes it as a "law". The uniformity of God's activities in his creation enables the scientist to predict the course of natural phenomena. The trustworthiness of God's behaviour in his world is the foundation of all scientific truth. Upon it the scientist rests his faith and from there he goes on to achieve great and useful things in such fields as those of navigation, chemistry, agriculture, and the medical arts.'[1]

• A true perspective

As Christians we need to see beyond these impersonal laws to the hand of God. God's power is real and omnipotence is a real attribute of God. If we forget this we shall be in serious trouble. For too long we have allowed the world's secularised mentality to colour our views of God. Consequently the sovereign, omnipotent God of Scripture has become a helpless, feeble God, who can only do what we allow. We have emptied God of omnipotence and replaced it with sentiment.

This inevitably affects our views of Jesus. In modem Christianity Jesus is often a sad, pathetic figure standing out in the cold, begging to come in. This is typified in Holman Hunt's painting *The Light of the World.* But this is not the Jesus of Scripture; he walked on water, calmed the storm, raised the dead and commands all men everywhere to repent. Somehow or other we have lost sight of Jesus who is mighty to save. We confess to the same faith and to believing the same doctrines as Spurgeon and Whitefield, but do we have any acquaintance at all with the almighty God whom they knew so intimately?

• Encouragement

The power of God works for his people and through his people. Tozer wrote, 'The church began in power, moved in power and moved just as long as she had power. When she no longer had power she dug in for safety and sought to conserve her gains. But her blessings were like manna; when they tried to keep it over night it bred worms and stank... In church history every return to New Testament power has marked a new advance somewhere, a fresh proclamation of the Gospel, an upsurge of missionary zeal; and every diminution of power has seen the rise of some new mechanism for conservation and defence.'[1]

These words of Tozer bring us a serious warning but also great encouragement. The Christian church today seems so weak and powerless, and this discourages Christians in their attempts to serve the Lord. Our lack of power puts us on the defensive, but that must be wrong. An awareness of powerlessness ought to turn us in desperation to the omnipotent God who, time and time again, has worked in power in his church. This does not mean that we do nothing until God comes in power, but it encourages us to trust God as we seek to serve him.

☐ We need a deeper conviction of the authority of scripture

Believing the Bible has traditionally meant, for evangelical Christians, accepting it as the inspired, inerrant Word of God. This is far more than believing that the Bible contains the Word of God. For the evangelical the Bible is God's Word. Because of its unique qualities it is the supreme authority for what we believe and the way we live our lives.

Much has been written on what the words *inspired* and *inerrant* mean, and I do not wish to add to that in this chapter other than briefly to define their meaning. *Inspired* means that those who actually wrote the sixty-six books of the Bible did not give their own opinion but were guided and directed by the Holy Spirit – '...men spoke from God as they were carried along by the Holy Spirit' (2 Peter 1:21). In the words of E. J. Young, *inerrant* means that 'the Scriptures possess the quality of freedom from error. They are exempt from the liability of mistake, incapable of error. In all their teachings they are in perfect accord with the truth.'

If the Bible is both inspired and inerrant, it must inevitably be the Christian's supreme authority for what they believe and how they live. The believer's great concern must be to please God, and to live for the glory of God. The Bible tells us how to do this, because in his book God declares his will for our lives. If we really accept the authority of the Bible, we will test everything by what the Scriptures say. This is why it is so important for Christians both to know and believe their Bible.

If the Bible is not our authority, then something else will be, and in all probability it will be our own human understanding. The choice is then between what I think and what God has said. To make our own opinion our authority is really a most flimsy foundation on which to build.

In recent years there have been two major shifts in the thinking of evangelicals towards the Bible. Some no longer wholeheartedly accept the inspiration of Scripture, and that undermines any claim that the Bible exercises real authority in their lives. Others, whilst still accepting an orthodox doctrine of Scripture, in actual fact deny by their lives what they say they believe. These two attitudes have been around for a long time (see 2 Timothy 4:3-4; Titus 1:15-16), but in recent years they have been more pronounced.

• No authority

If there is no supreme authority there can be no absolute standards and everything becomes relative. Nothing is right, nothing is wrong; it just depends upon how each individual sees things. So in the world there are no longer any moral standards, and in the church there are no longer any absolute truths. For instance, it is clear from the New Testament that the church in the first century believed in the reality of hell, but today if you believe this you are considered to be very strange, rather outdated and certainly lacking in love.

There is a very clear link between the morals of the world and the lack of doctrinal certainty of the church. When the church has to debate whether or not it should conduct marriage services for homosexuals, it is not only rejecting the biblical teaching but is also encouraging sin. Very often the reason given for such discussion is that we should love and not condemn. This sounds very laudable, but basically it is a flawed argument. For instance, no one loved like Jesus, but some of his condemnations in Scripture are scathing. He called the religious leaders of his day a brood of vipers (Matthew 23:33), and he said that some of them belonged to the devil (John 8:44).

Because the Bible is so often rejected today, we have a very confused understanding of what love is. It is not loving to mislead people by saying that everyone is going to heaven if God, in his Word, very clearly says this is not so. The same is true in the moral realm. A young woman falls in love with a man. They begin seeing each other, and before long they are sleeping together. She speaks passionately of how much she loves him, but when confronted with the fact that he is married and has three children, all she can say is, 'I know, but I cannot help it. I love him.' What has this so-called love to do with the love spoken of in 1 Corinthians 13 There, love 'is not self-seeking' and 'does not delight in evil'. Clearly there is no relationship between the two. One 'love' destroys a marriage and brings untold misery to three children, while the other 'always protects, always trusts, always hopes, always perseveres'.

It is not possible to reject the authority of Scripture and still hold on to a moral code that takes the commands of God seriously. The world may call it old-fashioned and narrow-minded to believe the Bible, but the results of not believing are seen all around us in the breakdown of family life and the moral mess that characterises life at the beginning of the twenty-first century.

• Tolerating sin

Evangelical Christians today tolerate what they would have rejected forty years ago. It is not that this toleration stems from a more generous spirit; it is, rather, the result of not adhering, as they once did, to the teaching of Scripture. To tolerate what God denounces is a recipe for disaster. Examples of this toleration abound in our attitude towards the Lord's Day; the breakdown of marriages of Christians; the number of evangelical ministers guilty of adultery; what we allow our children to watch on TV. The list is long and frightening.

It is true that years ago the behaviour pattern of evangelicals was dictated by tradition as well as Scripture. It may be that we were too narrow in some areas of our lives and these things needed dealing with, but today we seem to have thrown out the baby with the bath water. If the boast of the Pharisee was that he was not like other men, it seems that today many evangelicals boast that they are exactly like other men. This inverted Pharisaism stems directly from an attitude to Scripture that is not worthy of a person who claims to love the Lord Jesus Christ.

The Bible teaches that Christians are totally different from anyone else. Their standing before God is different — they are justified not condemned; their eternal destination is different – they are going to heaven not hell; and their life-style should be different. Paul writing to the Ephesians says, 'I ... insist on it in the Lord, that you must no longer live as the Gentiles do...' (Ephesians 4:17). Most of the rest of the letter following this verse tells us how the Lord expects his people to live. The detail of these instructions can leave no Christian uncertain as to what is expected of them. 'For you were once darkness, but now you are light in the Lord. Live as children of light...' (5:8). The apostle then goes on to say in verse 10 that the crucial thing for the believer is to '...find out what pleases the Lord'.

There is only one place to find out what pleases the Lord, and that is in the Bible. If we do not believe the Bible we are left with our own inward desires. Our thinking will be moulded, not by the will of God, but by some godless newspaper editor or trendy TV producer. The only way to live like a Christian is to think like a Christian, and the only way to think like a Christian is to spend more time listening to what God is saying in his Word. This is why we should believe and live by the Bible.

Without the Bible we have nothing to say to the world that is any different from the moral, and in some cases immoral, platitudes that come from the lips of men who do not know God. We have no substitute for Scripture. An evangelicalism that proclaims the love of God but at the same time avoids the basic New Testament teaching on sin, guilt and judgement, and the need for repentance, is an evangelicalism that is sending souls to hell. It is impossible to be saved without repentance; repentance is not possible without conviction of sin and there will be no conviction unless men and women are confronted with their sin. Why believe the Bible? Let A. W. Tozer have the last word:

'Within the circles of evangelical Christianity itself there have arisen in the last few years dangerous and dismaying trends away from true Bible Christianity. A spirit has been introduced which is surely not the Spirit of Christ, methods employed which are wholly carnal, objectives adopted which have not one line of scripture to support them, a level of conduct accepted which is practically identical with that of the world – and yet scarcely one voice has been raised in opposition. And this in spite of the fact that the Bible-honouring followers of Christ lament among themselves the dangerous, wobbly course things are taking. So radically is the essential spirit and content of orthodox Christianity changing these days under the vigorous leadership of undiscerning religionists that, if the trend is not stopped, what is called Christianity will soon be something altogether other than the faith of our fathers. We'll have only Bible words left. Bible religion will have perished from wounds received in the house of her friends. The times call for a Spirit-baptised and articulate orthodoxy.'[1]

□ We need a more biblical love for Jesus

Love for Jesus is not some sentimental emotion. If that is all it is, it will be shallow and pliable. It will be unable to stand in times of stress and trials. Several years ago I heard a young woman give a testimony of salvation. She said she had been in love with a young man and when he finished the relationship she was heart-broken. Some one took her to a church and there she heard about Jesus. She said that she now loved Jesus and that he was her new boy friend. I felt deeply sorry for this young woman. She was obviously sincere but her understanding of Jesus and salvation was tragically very shallow. I was left wondering what would happen to Jesus when a new boy friend came along.

• God's love for us

Our love for Jesus is a response to God's love for us. The apostle John says, 'This is love; not that we loved God but that he loved us and sent his Son as an atoning sacrifice for our sins.' (1John 4:10).

The Bible has a great deal to say about the love of God, but do we really understand the exact meaning of 'divine love'? Several years ago, I was preaching on the love of God at a baptismal service. One of those being baptised was a young woman who had persuaded her father to attend. He rarely, if ever, went to church, and when his daughter asked him what he thought of the sermon, he answered that it was the same old stuff about the love of God. His thinking was, 'What was so special about God's love? Isn't that what He is supposed to do? It's the same old stuff.' The poor man could not have been more wrong. The love of God is the most amazing thing there is. Every Christian knows something of the wonder of Paul's words in Galatians 2:20, that Jesus '...loved me and gave himself for me.' This love is not sentiment or an empty gesture; rather, it does something very definite.

In Romans 5:6-8 Paul is concerned that we fully understand what God's love means. After mentioning it in verse five, he proceeds in verses six to eight to define it in what must be one of the great New Testament statements on divine love. 'You see, at just the right time, when we were still powerless, Christ died for the ungodly. Very rarely will anyone die for a righteous man, though for a good man someone might possibly dare to die. But God demonstrates his own love for us in this; While we were still sinners, Christ died for us.' There can be no true understanding of God's love apart from the cross.

There is nothing vague or undetermined about God's love. The words 'at just the right time' speak of the eternal nature of this love. It was planned in eternity and worked out to a divinely appointed timetable. Christ's death on the cross was totally planned by God. Divine love didn't originate at Bethlehem when Jesus was born, but it stretched back before the creation of the world. There had been many tokens of this love to men and women, but the cross was the most glorious demonstration possible, especially when we realise who are the objects of God's love. In Romans five, Paul describes the recipients of this amazing love as powerless, ungodly and sinners.

A sinful, powerless, ungodly person comes to experience God's love by faith in the Lord Jesus Christ. Jesus is the one and only Son of God. He is the delight of the Heavenly Father. Jesus came into a sinful world yet never sinned. But this Jesus died for us. That is the depth of God's love. Paul, in illustrating divine love, points us not to the sinless life or teachings or miracles of Jesus, but to his death. He does this because this is how God demonstrates or proves his love for us.

The life of Jesus was perfect and holy and sinless, but it could not, on its own, save one single ungodly person. His teaching was amazing, and it was no exaggeration to say that no one ever spoke with his clarity and authority; but all the parables and 'Sermons on the Mount' could not help a man to salvation who is powerless. Christ's miracles were startling and there was no doubt of their genuineness, even his enemies acknowledged that; but all these events could not save a sinner from the guilt and penalty of sin. In order to save us, Christ had to die for us.

This was necessary for several reasons – one was the nature and power of sin. Its grip on human nature is total and its strength is death. It will take all to the grave, to death and to hell. If we are to be saved, that power has to be broken. On the cross, Jesus faced death for us. He faced it bearing our guilt and sin and He faced it in a weakness caused by Him being our substitute and sin-bearer. It was a weakness not known by Him before. In this state of weakness and humiliation, Jesus triumphed over death. He conquered it and abolished it for his people. The resurrection was the evidence of this great victory, and here we see again the wonder of God's love.

As Christians look at the cross and take in all we can of its meaning and accomplishment, it is breathtaking, thrilling and humbling. Such love should draw from us a love for the Saviour that supersedes all the other loves in our lives.

• Our love for God

If we love Jesus, we are left in no doubt what he expects from us – 'If you love me, you will obey what I command' (John 14:15). Love means obedience and submission to the will of God. We tend to think of love as a response of the heart and obedience as a response of the will; but Jesus says this is not so. Love is not a feeling but an act of obedience. Love, of course, is not divorced from feeling because the obedience required from us is not a forced grudging act, but a cheerful and happy response of God's love for us.

John Brown says, 'If I love Christ, I shall keep his commandments cheerfully; I shall reckon it a privilege to obey his law, "to be under the law to Christ". The thought, that they are the commandments of him whom I love, because of his excellences and his kindness, makes me love his law, for it must be excellent because it is his, and it must be fitted to promote my happiness for the same reason. And I have pleasure in pleasing him, and I am pained when I am aware of having offended him; and, therefore, I have satisfaction in doing what I am sure will please him, for he has commanded it.'[2]

More love for Jesus would solve most of our church problems. It would see the end of half-hearted Christianity. It would rid us of the attitude of mind that only plays at evangelicalism. A serious commitment would be inevitable if we loved Jesus as we ought to. Gone also would be most of the niggling criticisms and small mindedness that is part of so many churches.

☐ We need a growing love for all believers

In his first letter the apostle John has some very strong things to say about Christians loving one another – 'Dear friends, let us love one another, for love comes from God. Every one who loves has been born of God and knows God. Whoever does not love God does not know God, because God is love' ... 'If anyone says, I love God, yet hates his brother, he is a liar. For anyone who does not love his brother, whom he has seen, cannot love God, whom he has not seen. And he has given us this command; Whoever loves God must also love his brother.' (1 John 4:7-8; 20-21).

If the Christian life were to be symbolised as a tree; love would be its roots, its trunk, its branches and most of its leaves. Without love everything else is nothing (1 Corinthians 13:1-3). Without love our doctrines would sooner or later cause us to persecute, either verbally or physically, those who do not agree with us. Without love our lives have no purpose, direction or substance. We are a sham. John puts it more bluntly and says we are liars.

To love fellow Christians is a must for every believer. True, it is not easy but it is essential. How can we love those Christians who are as selfish, arrogant and envious as we are? It is hard, especially when we read in 1 Corinthians 13:4-7 what this love involves – 'Love is patient, love is kind. It does not envy, it does not boast, it is not proud. It is not rude, it is not self-seeking, it is not easily angered, it keeps no record of wrongs. Love does not delight in evil but rejoices with the truth. It always protects, always trusts, always hopes, always perseveres.'

Some Christians apply Paul's great chapter on love to Jesus and read it – Jesus is patient, Jesus is kind etc. That is true, but it is a completely wrong application of what

Paul is saying. He is not talking about Jesus in 1 Corinthians 13 but about Christians, and particularly those caught up in controversy as the Corinthians Christians were.

Dr. Lloyd-Jones commenting on 1 John 2:7-11 writes, '...The Lord Jesus Christ has made it possible for us to keep this commandment in an entirely new manner. John is here reminding them that they are left without excuse; it is possible now for Christians, as the result of receiving new life from Christ, as the result of the power of the Holy Spirit, to love their fellow men and women, to love their brethren in the way that God originally intended.[3]

• **Reasons to love**

There are very practical reasons why we ought to love our fellow believers. Church life would be transformed. Suspicion and criticism would disappear. Tension would be minimised and harmony of effort would replace it. However John gives us other reasons.

Firstly, we must love each other because God is love. God is the fountain out of which love flows – 'love comes from God.' If we claim to know God as our Heavenly Father then something of his nature of love must show in us.

Secondly, the prime action of God's love was to send his Son as an atoning sacrifice for our sins. Jesus is the gift of God's love to undeserving sinners. Because this is true we must love our brethren.

Thirdly, if we love each other we make God's love complete (verse 12). This does not mean that we improve upon it, that would be impossible, rather it means that we are fulfilling one of the purposes of God's love for us. In this way we bring that love to its completion.

James Montgomery Boice gives reasons why love is pre-eminent for the believer.

'...**The first reason** is obviously that we need love most, particularly in the so-called evangelical churches. These have sound doctrine, at least to a point. There is a measure of righteousness. But often, sadly, there is very little love. Without it, however, there is no true demonstration of the life of Christ within or true worship of the Father.

The second reason is that Jesus Himself made love the first and second of the commandments. The first commandment is love for God (Deuteronomy 6:4). The second is love for one another (Leviticus 19:18). The two properly belong together. As Jesus said, "All the Law and the Prophets hang on these two commandments" (Matthew 22:40).

The third reason is that it was the realisation of this double love in us for both God and man that was the object of Christ's coming. This is what John seems to speak about in the opening verses of the letter when he says, "We proclaim to you what we have seen and heard, so that you also may have fellowship with us. And our fellowship is with the Father and with his Son, Jesus Christ" (1:3). That is, the coming of Christ is proclaimed so that those who hear of His incarnation and death might believe in Him and thereby learn to love both God and one another.

The devil is the one who disrupts. The Lord Jesus Christ is the One who draws together. Moreover, in the drawing together into fellowship, love is the key factor. Little

surprise then that we have this commandment from Him:
"Whoever loves God must also love his brother."'[4]

Of John's three tests, love is the one above all that shows
that we really are Christ's people. Dr Lloyd-Jones says,
'...Let me put it like this; it is not our intellectual opinion
that proclaims truly what we are. You know, it is possible
for us to be perfectly orthodox but to be unloving. But your
orthodoxy is of no value to you if you do not love your
brother; you can talk about this doctrine intellectually, you
can be a defender of the faith, and yet the spirit in which
you are defending it may be denying the very doctrine you
are defending. This is a terrible test! Orthodoxy is essential,
but it is not enough. "If you are not loving your brother,"
says John in effect, "you are in darkness, you have not the
love of Christ." To love your brother is much more important than orthodoxy; yes, it is more important than mere
mechanical correctness in your conduct and behaviour in
an ethical sense. There are people who, like the rich young
ruler, can say, "All these things ..." They are not guilty of
the gross sins which they have seen in others, and yet their
spirit as they criticise is a portrayal that they do not love
their brother. Harshness, the criticising spirit – all that is a
negation of this spirit of love. It is something that rises up in
my heart and nature and it is, therefore, the proof positive
of whether I belong to Him or not. "If ye know these things,"
said the Lord Jesus Christ, "happy are ye if ye do them"
(John 13:17). "If I," he also said in effect, in the same passage, "whom you call Lord and Master, have washed your
feet, how much more in a sense ought you to wash one
another's feet and be loving towards one another and be

anxious to serve one another." This thing is inevitable – if we belong to Him, we must be manifesting this spirit and type of life.'[5]

☐ We need to feel for the condition of the lost

We must be concerned for the souls of men and women because without Christ as their Saviour they are going to hell. They are not simply going to a 'Christless eternity' as it is often put. They are without Christ now and are going to exist for ever under the wrath and judgement of a holy God. Christians often ask, 'How can I get a burden for souls?' The answer has to be; read the Bible and believe it. Believe what it has to say about the wrath of the Lord and the eternity of judgement. This is what your unbelieving children and friends will have to face unless they turn to Christ. If that does not give you a burden for souls then nothing will. If unbelievers are to avoid hell they must be saved.

In recent years, much evangelistic effort has been so man-centred that it has produced countless 'decisions for Christ' but few true conversions to Christ. A method that does not see souls truly saved, but merely attracts and entertains sinners, is not biblical evangelism. The purpose of evangelism is to reach sinners with the gospel, so that they might come in repentance and faith to Christ.

One of the problems of the man-centred methods over the last forty years is that some Christians have been put off from doing any evangelism at all. Evangelical believers tend to swing from one extreme to another. We see bad, unbiblical methods being used and decide the safest thing to do is nothing. This attitude is just as wrong as a preoccupation with instant results. 'No evangelism' is not the answer to 'bad evangelism'.

• A lack of concern

Do we care enough for the souls of men and women, or are we indifferent to their salvation? Do we really believe in hell? If one of us had a young child in our family with some terminal illness we would be terribly grieved. We would feel the matter deeply and be unable to put it out of our minds. This is right and proper; it is a response governed by love and real concern. We would get our Christian friends to pray for the loved one and plead with God for healing. Physical death is real to us all and we feel its pangs and pain. But somehow eternal death is not so real to us. We all have loved ones who are living without Christ and who will go to hell if they die in that condition, but we rarely shed a tear for their souls. As long as the death of the body seems more important to us than spiritual death, evangelism will always lack the urgency that characterizes New Testament life and witness. This is not to say that the believer should become depressed over the state of the unsaved, for he should be filled with 'joy and peace in believing'. But there should be a godly concern for the lost.

• Past failures

The beginning of the twenty first century is a hard time for biblical Christianity and this has created in believers an acute sense of disappointment with past evangelistic efforts. The sentiments of many are: 'What is the use of telling sinners about Jesus when no one will listen? We see so few conversions that we have stopped expecting them.'

In many ways this attitude is understandable and one sympathizes with the disappointment of Christians frustrated with their past failures. But those who think in this way are forgetting the sovereignty of God and revealing an ignorance of church history. So often in the past, times of acute spiritual darkness have been followed by times of rich blessing. What a dark time it was for Israel with that wicked man Herod on the throne. Their God-given land was ruled by the armies of pagan Rome, and their God-given religion was being sucked dry by the legalism and pride of the Pharisees! To any godly soul the situation must have seemed dark and hopeless. Yet at that very moment God sent Jesus into the world.

The same lesson has been evident all through the history of the church. In 1721 Erasmus Saunders wrote *A View of the State of Religion in the Diocese of St David's.* He said that in West Wales, 'So many of our churches are in actual ruins; so many more are almost ready to fall.'[6]

Saunders went on to say that some men ordained to the church were practically illiterate, and far from being spiritually called, had entered the ministry because they were unlikely to succeed in any other profession. Growing up not far from St Davids at this awful time were nine-year-old Daniel Rowland and eight-year-old Howell Harris, and within a short time God used these young men to turn the land upside down spiritually. What God did then he can do again: times of little response are no reason to suspend the work of the gospel, but should instead prompt a greater sense of urgency.

• Telling the good news

In Acts 11:19-20 the evangelism of the early church is very simply described as telling the people 'the good news about the Lord Jesus'. They preached, proclaimed, heralded, declared, or stated the truth about Jesus. There was no hesitation, nor was the message watered down. Their evangelism was not half-hearted or reluctant. They believed that without Jesus people would go to hell, and this added a note of urgency to their message. But they also believed that before time began God, in love and mercy, had purposed to save a great multitude that no man could number. This added a note of joy and confidence to their message.

The early church was a telling church. Why was this? Were not music and drama available as means of communication in the society of their day? Yes, but telling or preaching was God's way of communicating the gospel – and it still is. The principle presented in Romans 10:14-15 is still relevant; how can they believe unless they hear, and how can they hear without someone preaching to them?

Somehow we have come to believe that telling or preaching the good news about Jesus is the work of the pulpit, while personal evangelism consists primarily in sharing our testimony with unbelievers. It must be good for Christians to give their testimony to non-Christians, but unless that testimony is accompanied by a clear, even if simple, declaration of who Jesus is and what he has done for sinners, then the testimony will have the wrong effect. It will make men look at us, rather than to Christ, or else our story will be dismissed as some mystical experience: 'That's fine for you, but not relevant for me.' It is the truth about Jesus that puts men and women 'on the spot' and forces them to think seriously about themselves and God. Even though all Christians cannot be preachers in the pulpit sense, we are all meant to tell the good news about the Lord Jesus.

• A passionate obsession

From 1 Corinthians 9:19 to the end of the chapter it is not difficult to see that Paul had a passionate obsession to win souls. Five times he uses the verb 'to win', which implies striving, discipline and effort, before (in verse 22) he changes it to 'save'. At stake was not the success or failure of a methodology but man's eternal destiny. Paul was concerned with success in evangelism, but not to further his reputation as a preacher; rather, he longed to see souls saved. He also felt under a solemn obligation to tell the gospel to all men. 'I am bound', he asserts, 'both to Greeks and non-Greeks, both to the wise and foolish. That is why I am so

eager to preach the gospel also to you who are at Rome'
(Romans 1:14-15).

This is why he approaches the task of evangelism with
such passion and vigour. Do we? So often we evangelize
because we feel we should and because we have to live up
to our name as 'evangelicals'. It then becomes a mere duty,
with the emphasis upon ourselves, not the unbeliever. Do
we have the time? Can we fit it in? Will it be inconvenient?
How much will it cost? We become more concerned with
methods that suit us than with the lost souls of men and
women. We are more concerned with our rights than our
responsibilities. We become afraid that if we do something
new or different we may violate the party line and bring
the criticism of other churches upon ourselves.

Paul was prepared to break all his religious traditions in
order to win those who were totally beyond the reach of
normal religious connections. His God-given, passionate
obsession compelled him to take seriously Christ's
command, not only to preach the gospel, but by doing so
to win souls and make disciples.

• Understanding the unbelievers mind

We were all unbelievers once but we quickly forget what
that was like. Add to that the fact that things have changed
drastically in attitudes to Christianity over the past twenty
years and it is not difficult to see how we have moved from
a general indifference to open hostility to the gospel. It has
always been true that the devil blinds people's minds to
the gospel, but the unbelievers of today are not those of

twenty or thirty years ago. There is a difference. Then it was fairly normal to go to church; now it is not. It can involve a culture-shock for unbelievers to enter a church. They feel out of place, uncomfortable and awkward.

We have to remember also that modern man's mind is largely conditioned by the media, with very negative attitudes to the church. Silly vicars in TV plays or outrageous public statements from bishops do not give Christianity a good press. Coupled with this is the un-scriptural, sentimental, almost humanistic trash that is frequently promulgated in the name of Christianity in religious broadcasts. All this is enough to put anyone off the gospel. Add to this Religious Education in schools, often taught by unbelievers and based on the premise that all religions are equally valid, and we see that the mind of modern man is conditioned to reject biblical Christianity.

What is the answer to all this? Clearly, as Christians, we are encouraged that salvation is 'of the Lord'. It is all of grace and there is no substitute in evangelism for the power of the Holy Spirit. But God works through us and our approach should be summed up in two words: love and reality.

People today don't trust others as they once did. They do not trust politicians. They do not trust business people or commercial advertising. They have become cynical and expect to be cheated, and react accordingly in their attitudes and relationships. They need to be weaned from their suspicion by seeing that we love them and care for them. Love has to be shown in all sorts of practical ways. You will never reach your neighbours with the gospel if the only time you speak to them is to invite them to church.

Many believers have very few friends who are not Christians? There are several reasons for this. When we were saved we were changed and some unbelieving friends, not being able to understand this change, cut us off. We also, on our part, may have cut off unbelieving friends, because their habits and interests were inconsistent with following Christ. Clearly, believers are not to be 'of the world'. But we remain in the world, and to cut off all friendships with non-Christians is, in evangelistic terms, disastrous. If we are uncomfortable with them, they will feel uncomfortable with us, and there will be little possibility of influencing them. Love for the lost means involvement with them, though not of course with their sins.

Then there is reality. Non-Christians need to see that our faith is real and meaningful to us. They are constantly watching us and looking to see how we cope as Christians with sickness, death, frustration, disappointment and sorrow. It is no use telling someone how wonderful it is to be a Christian, what joy and peace and satisfaction you have in Christ, and then reacting as the world reacts when troubles come. A consistent Christian walk is a powerful aid to evangelism. Without reality in life, all our professions of faith in Christ will ring hollow. Paul tells Titus that believers should 'adorn the doctrine of God our Saviour in all things' (Titus 2:10, AV).

□ We need a passionate desire to please God

The New Testament is always concerned with what pleases God and this is particularly true of the Epistle to the

Romans. Salvation is thought of as God accepting man and not as man accepting God. Therefore justification by faith becomes central to salvation. Sinners are saved on God's terms not theirs.

It is impossible to understand Romans apart from how Paul uses the word 'righteous'.

The gospel is about righteousness. 'For in the gospel a righteousness from God is revealed...' (1:17).

Man has no righteousness. '..There is no one righteous, not even one.' (3:10).

Salvation is God's righteousness imputed to us. 'But now a righteousness from God, apart from law, has been made known, to which the Law and the Prophets testify. This righteousness from God comes through faith in Jesus Christ to all who believe...' (3:21-22).

• Imputed righteousness

When we became Christians, God covered us in the right-eousness of Christ (Romans 3:21,22; 5:17; 10:3-11). In the Authorised Version of the Bible this righteousness is described as *imputed*, and in the New International Version as *credited*. Read Romans 4:18-25

Isaiah has a lovely picture of this: 'I delight greatly in the Lord; my soul rejoices in my God. For he has clothed me with garments of salvation and arrayed me in a robe of righteousness...' (Isaiah 61:10). Before we became Christians, how delighted we were with our own righteousness! how proud we were of our efforts! We thought, 'I am as good as anyone. Who can tell me I am a sinner?' The robe of self-righteousness fitted well and we loved it, until God showed us the perfect, sinless purity of Jesus and said, '...all our righteous acts are like filthy rags...' (Isaiah 64:6). Before long we too saw them as filthy rags, and we felt guilty and convicted of sin. Our problem was then; where could we find another robe to replace our discredited robe of self-righteousness? God answered, 'Come to me and I will clothe you in the garment of salvation.' When we came to God in repentance and faith, what did we find? Not a judge to condemn us, not one to mock our efforts and shame us in our guilt, but a loving heavenly Father, full of grace and compassion and mercy. He took us to his wardrobe of sovereign grace and brought out the robe of righteousness. We saw the price tag – 'purchased by the blood of Jesus' – and we noticed in amazement that it already had our name on it. It was fitted by the Holy Spirit and was perfect. Then, like Isaiah, we 'delighted greatly in the Lord' and rejoiced.

All this happened when we were saved. Righteousness was imputed (or credited) to us. Why did a soldier put on a breastplate when going into battle? Though he might have been as strong as an ox and superbly fit, he realised, for all that, his natural body could not withstand a spear, sword or arrow. So he covered himself with another body, a much stronger one – a breastplate. His protection then was not in him but upon him. In the same way our breastplate, our protection, is the imputed righteousness of God.

• Imparted righteousness

Thank God for imputed righteousness, but it is not an end in itself. There is also imparted righteousness. Having been saved by grace and covered with the imputed righteousness of God, the Holy Spirit of God now begins to work within us to change or to sanctify us. Gradually our thinking, our desires and our outlook on life all begin to change. We will never be sinless in this world, but we find ourselves beginning to hate sin. What is happening? This is imparted righteousness. The righteousness which in our salvation was not ours, but covered us like a robe, is now becoming a part of us. We begin to grow in grace and a knowledge of God.

The difference between imputed righteousness and imparted righteousness is that imputed righteousness is all Christ's, and is perfect and absolute. It covers us and makes us acceptable to God. Imparted righteousness is the Holy Spirit making us more like Jesus. It is the continual work of God within us, and whilst in this life it will never make us perfect, it does make us more Christlike. It is this imparted righteousness that makes us hate all that the devil stands for. We are new creatures with a new Lord and Master, and we fight evil.

Paul is concerned that we should know more and more of imparted righteousness because it is this that pleases God – 'Therefore, I urge you, brothers, in view of God's mercy, to offer your bodies as living sacrifices, holy and pleasing to God – this is your spiritual act of worship.' (Romans 12:1).

Paul wrote Romans to Christians he had never met. The letter was written from Corinth about AD57, 3 years before he went to Rome. It was written to a church that had not been in existence very long, probably only about 15 years. But he was concerned that these Christians should not only be acceptable to God because of Christ's righteousness imputed to them, but that they should also please God as their lives reflected the beauty of Christ as a result of imparted righteousness.

The Christian needs to ask himself every day if his life is pleasing to God? In Romans 12 Paul tells us what sort of life God delights in. He begins with the word 'therefore' – in the light of all he has been saying in chapters 1-11. Particularly he is concerned about our response to God's mercy, and this means our response to God's great blessing of justification. Without this being our experience, the apostle could never have said what he does in verses 12:1-2.

• I urge you

This is a strong plea but why does Paul have to use such language? He does it because all too often Christians are satisfied with being saved and make little effort to grow in their faith. You can test yourself on this. Have you grown spiritually in the past year? Are you concerned to please God at every point of your life? It is because we fail here that so many God-given gifts lay waste. Indifference and lack of commitment make us spiritual whimps instead of soldiers of the Lord. The Bible never does a deal with us. It never offers us a compromise but demands all we have and are.

• Offer your bodies as living sacrifices

We need to compare this with the sacrifices of the Old Testament. There the sacrifices were dead bodies of animals that were of no real use to God. But with the living sacrifice of committed Christians God can turn the world upside down.

The idea of 'body', means our total being – not merely our hands and feet, not just our heart and mind, but all that we are. Have you ever daydreamed of being a great preacher or missionary working for God in some far land? God does not want our daydreams because they are useless and accomplish nothing. You actually do nothing, apart from dream, and so God does not want our daydreams. He wants our bodies. He wants all we are and then perhaps our daydreams will become realities.

A disembodied, theoretical commitment is not biblical. What pleases God is the giving of ourselves totally and unreservedly to the work of the gospel. A very definite change of living will take the place of just wishful thinking.

• Do not conform any longer to the pattern of this world

Conforming is very easy and is often the reason why worldliness is so common among Christians. The spiritual nonconformity Paul demands is not automatic for the believer. The temptation to conform to the world's standard is always there and has to be fiercely resisted. It is not easy, but it is vital. If you want your car to run properly you do

not put water in the petrol tank. Why not? It is easier and
cheaper. It is also safer and it is certainly more pleasant in
taste and smell. In every way it is more convenient. All this
is true, but the presence of water in the petrol tank is alien
to the efficiency of the engine. It simply does not work.

This is also true of worldliness in the Christian's life. It
may be easier and less costly, it may be more convenient,
but it doesn't work. It clogs, slows down progress and eventually grinds us to a halt – so do not conform.

There is no doubt that in recent years there has been a
marked decline in commitment to the work of the gospel
among evangelical Christians. We can dress up worldliness
in spiritual garb and say we are being more tolerant and
less narrow minded, but worldliness is still sin and the
results are to be seen in the spiritual poverty of the church.

• Be transformed by the renewing of your mind

The concept of 'mind', means the spirit, intellect and heart
– the inner man. The believer needs to have his mind transformed to God's ways. Merely knowing God's ways are
not enough. We need to think the ways of God. We need
to think biblically and this means we must spend more time
in the Bible.

Sanctification does not just happen. You must work at it
and make it happen. You strive, labour, wrestle and weep.
You do not give in, but keep going despite failures and
disappointments. This is the way to please God. It is the
way to turn our daydreams into realities.

Christian, have you ever tried it?

8.
The New Testament Church

The past 40 years have been difficult ones for the church. In 1960 it was normal for evangelicals to attend church twice on Sunday; now some believe think it is enough if they only attend the morning service. Many began to reject the idea of church membership, arguing that having your name on a list was unbiblical and unnecessary. There had always been those who held to the view that you did not have to go to church to be a Christian, but the idea has grown in popularity. All in all the concept of 'church' is taking a battering.

We need to remember that the idea of church was not the invention of men but that God imposed it upon the first believers. The Lord, even in the Old Testament, was concerned that those who came into a living experience of him should also be in a living experience of each other. The Acts of the Apostles presents us with a picture of the developing early church and it is a picture almost unrecognisable today.

If you ask someone today to describe a church, the answers would be varied, depending upon whom you ask. They would reveal a confusion of thought and understanding and would bear no resemblance to the church of the New Testament. The confusion arises because we fail to ask another question first – what is a Christian? The two questions are inseparably linked. The church will only be what its members are. If they are just religious people with no experience of regeneration then the church will be little more than a social club. But if they are true Christians, as defined by scripture, then the church should reflect something of what we see in the New Testament.

If you want one word to sum up the first church members in the New Testament, it would be 'life.' They were spiritually alive and therefore their church was alive. Their Christianity vibrated with life. There is, however, a difference between *life* and *lively*. A church can be lively in the sense that it has plenty of activities, but at the same time be devoid of true spiritual life. So we need to ask what sort of life does God want to see in his church? The answer to this is found in Acts 2.

☐ A confessing life (verse 4)

The life of the church is always dependent upon the indwelling power of the Holy Spirit. We read that they were all filled with the Holy Spirit. The confessing, witnessing and proclaiming of their faith was not left to the man in the pulpit. They all confessed to the grace of God in Christ. When a church believes that if the preaching is sound then everything is all right, it is failing to be a New Testament church. The tendency with such thinking is that it enjoys sermons and does little or nothing else, whereas in the New Testament all the church members were involved in spreading the gospel.

In verse 4 we see that they were enabled by the Spirit. If there is no Holy Spirit, there will be no power, no life, and no confession. Note what they spoke of – 'the wonders of God' (verse 11). What is our main topic of conversation? The answer to this will tell us whether we know anything of the filling of the Holy Spirit.

☐ A convicting life (verse 7 & 12)

Such was the reality of Christ and the Holy Spirit in the lives of these Christians that unbelievers were startled and amazed. They saw a difference and that difference was Christ. When people saw this they began to ask questions: 'Are not all these men who are speaking Galileans?' In other words they said, 'these are just ordinary folk, the same as us, yet there is a difference. What does this mean?' They could not dismiss what they were hearing and they wanted an explanation.

Is this the sort of reaction we get from unbelievers today? Lives in Acts 2 were touched, and hearts were convicted by what they saw and heard. This is a crucial part of evangelism. People will not listen to us if they cannot see Christ in us.

☐ A converting life (verse 37 & 41)

The result of this Holy Spirit activity *in* the lives of Christians was that a huge crowd were prepared to listen to Peter preach and as a consequence 3,000 were saved. Do we believe this sort of thing could happen today? If we were honest we would have to say no. We have no expectation of one being saved let alone many. This is because conversions are few and far between these days, but more importantly it is because we have little experience of Spirit power in our lives and in our churches.

There is no substitute for Christians filled with the Holy Spirit and by this we do not mean the extraordinary manner of tongues speaking that we see in Acts 2, but the filling of the Spirit that Paul refers to in Ephesians 5:18. There he speaks of the Spirit filled life that is needed to be a good husband, wife, parent and child. This filling is crucial to leading a normal Christian life as defined in the New Testament.

☐ A consistent life (verse 42 & 46a)

Here is something that is so lacking in today's evangelicals – consistency. These were no flash in the pan conversions. These were no hot and cold Christians – enthusiastic one day but bored and indifferent the next. These were no 'pick our meeting, pick our preacher', Christians.

Their consistency is seen in that they devoted themselves every day to the things of God. This consistency was based firmly upon doctrine, fellowship, sacrament and prayer. Because of this solid foundation the church was not pushed off track by adverse circumstances. The church today is full of good starters, but where are the finishers, the consistent ones. These early Christians were not super-saints but very ordinary men and women. They were not perfect but they were reliable. The life they lived was consistent with the doctrine they believed. Their fellowship was consistent – every day – and this was only possible because there was a deep bond of love between them.

Fellowship is something that has to be worked at rather than some emotional feeling. We need to remember that the church consists of sinners. It is true that they are sinners saved by grace but none the less they are still far from perfect. One of the major problems in church life is that we forget this. We set too low a standard for ourselves and too high a standard for others. We expect more from them than we are prepared to give ourselves. For instance, if folk in the church do not visit us when we are ill we get upset, but do we visit others when they have problems?

None of us are perfect in attitude or behaviour, so let us all exercise a little tolerance. This is not to excuse sin, but it will help us to be more consistent in our love for each other.

□ A contagious life (verse 47)

We talk of certain diseases as being contagious, but the most contagious thing this world can ever see is a church living a confessing, convicting, converting and consistent life. This is catching.

We are told the church 'enjoyed the favour of all the people'. This was because the life of the church was so different from normal religious and secular life. Most religions were a sham and secular life was a rat race, but these Christians exhibited a beautiful and joyous Christ centred life.

People today are looking for this reality and they ought to be able to see it in Christians. Our message is superb. It cannot be beaten, but sadly our lives let it down.

9.
Dealing with problems in the Church

There will always be problems in the church and this should not surprise us. It is part of the spiritual battle we have with the world, the flesh and the devil. This does not mean that we calmly accept the problems as if there is nothing we can do about them. In Ephesians 4:1-3 Paul shows us how to deal with our difficulties – 'As a prisoner for the Lord, then, I urge you to live a life worthy of the calling you have received. Be completely humble and gentle; be patient, bearing with one another in love. Make every effort to keep the unity of the Spirit through the bond of peace.'

In the first three chapters of Ephesians Paul has been teaching the doctrines of the Christian faith, but doctrine is not an end in itself. It is crucial, but it is not enough so Paul has to *urge* (4: 1) and *insist* (4:17) that we put the doctrine into practice. Do not be satisfied with knowing the truth. Your ambition ought to be to live the truth – exactly what Paul is saying in verse 1. Then immediately in verse 2 he tells us what this means.

Humility, gentleness, patience and love are the characteristics of the Christian life. These are all to do with our relationship with each other. If we are right with God then we ought to be right with God's people. It is the absence of humility, gentleness, patience and love in the church that cause tensions and quarrels and will inevitably lead to a lack of unity. When we were saved God put us in Christ. The Holy Spirit creates in all true believers a unity of being one in Christ. But if we do not live the life God expects of us we will break this unity. Paul urges us to make every effort to keep this unity by being humble, gentle, patient and loving.

Unity in the church has to be worked at. The tensions in churches between young and old believers can be devastating. Style of worship, type of hymns and songs, and versions of the Bible, can all shatter the unity of the Spirit if we fail to deal with them in humility, gentleness, patience and love.

When the New Testament talks of unity it does not mean uniformity. It is a unity based on the common belief in the doctrines of chapters 1-3, but there is more to it even than this. We are not told to be at unity only with those who believe exactly what we believe – that would be a very small church – but with those who are part of the one body (4:4).

Stuart Olyott says,' Do you sometimes look at other Christians and wonder how much you really have in common with them We are such an assorted bunch! We come from different backgrounds and nations; we vary in intellect, achievement, social status and wealth; we represent a whole spectrum of characters, hang-ups and eccentricities, and express widely contrasting likes and dislikes! There are so many differences between us. What really do we have in common? All the distinctions we have mentioned are temporary. But there are seven eternal realities which we possess in common with all believers everywhere. What we share is immeasurably greater than what differentiates us. It is not logical that we should live in any form of disunity.'[1]

The seven realities are spelt out in chapter 4 verses 4-6, one body, one Spirit, one hope, one Lord, one faith, one baptism, one God.

Christians have the same saving experience of the same Holy Spirit. One Lord has saved us and he has done so by giving us faith to believe in Christ. The phrase 'one baptism' causes some of us problems. Some will have been baptised by sprinkling of water as a child; others by immersion after they were saved – so there appears to be two baptisms. Because of this, baptism has become a great cause of disunity among Christians, but Paul is using it here as a reason for unity. This is because he is not talking about the mode or subject of baptism but the fact that baptism always signifies identification with Christ.

James Montgomery Boice said, 'that is the unifying thing. Have you been baptised into Christ? I do not care how you were baptised. I do not care whether it was in a baptistery or a stream, whether it was with a little bit of water or in a lot of water. Have you been publicly identified with Jesus Christ? That is the issue. And if that is the issue, then before the world we are identified together with Jesus Christ and must stand together for him.'[2]

All Christians do not have the same gifts and abilities (4:7&11). We are all different, yet the difference is not to effect our unity in Christ. Whatever gifts and abilities we have they are all to work to the common aim 'that the body of Christ may be built up' (4:12). God wants mature Christians whose lives reflect the beauty of Christ (4:13). The opposite of maturity is infancy and spiritual infancy is demonstrated by instability and gullibleness (4:14).

Spiritual infancy is not necessarily true only of young believers. It is nothing to do with age but with a doctrinal instability that leaves the believer open to all sorts of weird viewpoints. Their beliefs are not dictated by the word of God but by any current opinion that is doing the rounds, or even by what has always been done previously. We need to be checking this continually – are the issues I feel strongly about biblical and am I prepared to submit them to the final authority of God's word?

Tradition can be a very strong master in dictating present actions. We come to believe that the way we do things is the only way and we view other ways with suspicion. But this is nonsense. In the USA many churches stand when the Scriptures are read, but in Britain most congregations sit down for the reading. Who is right? The fact is neither is right or wrong. It is a matter of local custom and tradition. If the Scriptures commanded us to stand or sit for the reading of God's Word then it would be clear; but because there is no such command we have the freedom to do either.

In other words, there are matters and actions that are neither right or wrong and to insist that our way is the only way is evangelical pharaseeism. Again we need to be checking this continually – are the issues we feel strongly about biblical or are they merely tradition?

Growth in the church is the product of spiritual growth in each individual Christian. We all have a part to play in the well being of the church and we should be concerned that we promote growth not disunity. The teenagers in the church have as much a part to play in this as the older members.

Let us now come back to those four words in verse 2 of chapter 4 and see how they should effect our thinking and behaviour in times when the unity of the church is challenged by differences.

□ Humility

Differences cause us to take sides and defend a point of view. Then arrogance can easily be confused as strength and stubbornness as being firm. We have all done it. The only remedy is a humble spirit that is willing to consider the other point of view. Humility keeps its eye all the time on 4:3; '...keep the unity of the Spirit...', and verse 12, '...so that the body of Christ may be built up.' It refuses to attack people. It knows it has enough faults of its own. It is willing to admit when it makes mistakes.

□ Gentleness

This calms us into not getting aggressive or argumentative. It brings the spirit of Christ to bear on the problem and causes us to be meek but not weak; firm but not opinionated.

If we approach difficulties with gentleness, voices will not get raised in anger and a party spirit is resisted. Gentleness is self-controlled and it is lack of self-control that will shatter unity in a church.

□ Patience

This does not expect others to see things as you do but is willing to wait for views to change. Patience has won more battles than aggression ever will. Lack of patience can cause you to say things you later regret.

□ Love

Love is able to bear with those who disagree with you. It can take abuse from others while still loving them. How we need love in the church. It can deal with the sin of others, not in a judgmental way, but conscious that we are all sinners.

How desperately we need these qualities in the church. Do you have them? Test yourselves.

♦ If you disagree with someone, can you speak graciously with them about your difference – or do you only grumble about them to those who agree with you?

♦ Are you able to be flexible on matters that are not clearly biblical but only a matter of personal likes and dislikes?

♦ Is your spirit still sweet and in close fellowship with the Lord?

♦ Are you honestly making every effort to keep the unity of the Spirit and does the unity of the church matter to you?

We will never all agree on everything, but what is crucial is how we handle our differences. We can do so as Ephesians 4 says, or are our actions and words the same as a group of unregenerate men and women. Is our concern for the glory of God, or that we get our own way?

10.
Revival

In Psalm 85:6 the psalmist prays, 'Will you not revive us again, that your people may rejoice in you?' It is a prayer that has been since echoed by God's people on many occasions since. Having looked at evangelicalism in Britain during the second half of the 20th century and the beginning of the 21st, we must now surely be making the same plea to God.

☐ What is revival?

When the psalmist asked God for revival, what did he mean? What was he looking for? Revival implies life but God does not revive the dead because they need regeneration not revival. If a man is pulled unconscious out of the sea, someone may try to revive him with the kiss of life. But if the body has been in the sea for several days, then no one will try. The man is dead and revival is impossible.

So it is with spiritual revival. It is impossible to revive the spiritually dead. In other words, revival is a work of God among believers, among those who are already spiritually alive. The psalmist says revive us, not them.

Initially revival is not the answer to a godless society – it is the answer to a loveless and powerless church. A church filled with the power of the Holy Spirit is the answer to a godless society.

□ Why do we need reviving?

The answer to this question is because our spiritual life has declined. The causes for this are many but it always comes back to the same thing – sin. Worldliness, losing sight of our Saviour and departing from our first love, are all causes and they are all sin.

The saddest thing about this condition is that it is not unusual. This is why the psalmist has to say, 'revive us again'. It is the fact that declined spiritual life is not unusual that is its greatest danger. We can take the 'usual' to be the 'normal'. We get acclimatised to our condition and if it ever bothers us, we take comfort that all Christians are the same. We may be even spiritually better than most others, but what does this matter if we are powerless.

This was the trouble in the church at Sardis. It had a reputation of being alive and no doubt was proud of that, but in God's sight it was dead (Revelation 3:1-6). It was even worse at Laodicea, 'You say, I am rich; I have acquired wealth and do not need a thing. But you do not realise that you are wretched, pitiful, poor, blind and naked.' (Revelation 3:17). Churches like these never pray for revival because they see no need of it. The psalmist was different. He saw the need and hence the prayer. Do we see the need?

In Psalm 85 we are shown three reasons why we should cry to God for revival.

□ The anger of God is upon us (verses 3-5)

Divine anger is God's response to the sin of his people. The psalmist was very aware of this. He realised that the problems of a powerless people of God were not caused by satanic oppression but by divine wrath. God hates all sin and will not tolerate it especially when it is the sin of his own redeemed people. So the prayer for revival is a confession of guilt. If it is not, it will never be answered.

Our spiritual condition is our own fault. The cry for revival is a cry for mercy that God will bring us back to a place we have left, enticed away by sin. This is the tragedy of sin in a Christian, when it comes in, blessing goes out.

God's anger comes because he hates sin, but there is another reason – God loves his people. Divine anger is an expression of divine love. If this anger did not come to disturb our lives we would be content to live forever in a declining spiritual life. This is why the prayer for revival must include repentance and confession of sin.

Revival cannot be organised; it cannot be worked up – God alone can do it. It is not the result of prayer or preaching, but we must pray and preach. Revival is the result of the mercy of God. Revivals have nearly always produced great preaching, but great preaching cannot produce revival.

☐ The need for us to rejoice in the Lord (verse 6)

When God's people sin they cannot lose their salvation but they do lose many other things. Foremost among these is the joy of the Lord. This joy is not emotions whipped up to fever pitch. It is not even rejoicing in blessings from God, but rather is rejoicing in the Lord himself.

Scripture makes it abundantly clear that Christians are meant to rejoice in the Lord. 'Then will I go to the altar of God, to God, my joy and my delight...' (Ps 43:4).

In Psalm 63 David was up to his neck in trouble, but how different is his prayer from our formal and predictable petitions. Read the whole Psalm.

In Philippians 4:4 Paul tells us to rejoice in the Lord always. He was writing from a prison cell but even there his heart was warmed by the felt experience of the sheer goodness of God.

What do we know of these things? It is the poverty of our prayer life that exposes our lack of Christian joy. Our prayers become polite, correct, nice but powerless. Listen to Maurice Roberts,

'There is, however, the very real possibility in every Christian that they will learn to live at a distance from the love of Christ. Our corruption works in us a constant tendency to withdraw from Christ into the shadows. Days and even months can go past in the experience of the Lord's people, in which they are virtual strangers to the inward enjoyment of the love of Christ in their hearts. The soul grows callous. Layers of worldliness or coldness, like coats of paint on an old door, overspread the soul till we become

accustomed to feeling nothing, enjoying nothing, expecting nothing, knowing nothing of those heart-warmings
which are all-important to spiritual well-being. The next
step is that the believer falls into a dead formalism. Prayer
is got through as mere duty and routine. The Bible is read
either to keep up appearances or to salve the weak voice
of conscience. But spiritual exercises are now no longer
enjoyed. The soul has no relish for the things of the Spirit.
The consequence is that new companions are sought who
are unfriendly to heart-religion. Then corners are cut in
obedience to the Word of God.'[1]

This is why we need reviving. We are all aware that the
condition Roberts describes has gone on for too long in
our hearts. No joy of the Lord is a symptom of no felt presence of the Lord.

□ That glory may dwell in our land (verse 9)

If the glory of the Lord is not in his church then it cannot be
in the land. The frightening thing about sin in the Christian
is that it not only brings upon us God's anger, but God's
glory also departs. *Ichabod* (the glory is departed) is written today over so many churches in countries which were
previously known for their Christian character – thus those
countries know nothing of God.

Glory in the land means the presence of God is recognised and valued. The whole land may not be converted
but the glory of the Lord frustrates the activity of sin. You
can see this in Psalm 85, 'Love and faithfulness meet
together; righteousness and peace kiss each other. Faithfulness springs forth from the earth, and righteousness looks

down from heaven. The Lord will indeed give what is good, and our land will yield its harvest. Righteousness goes before him and prepares the way for his steps (verses 10-13).'

Revival deals firstly with believers but it does not stop there. Inevitably it goes on to touch unbelievers and multitudes are saved. Duncan Campbell describing the revival in the Hebrides between 1949-52 said, 'Revival is a going of God among his people, an awareness of God laying hold of the community … revival is a community saturated with God.'[2]

That is glory in the land.

When Psalm 85 was written the psalmist was not experiencing revival. On the contrary he acutely feels the wrath of God upon the people yet there is hope and confidence expressed at the end of the Psalm.

Is this justified or is it wishful thinking? The Psalmist has a real basis for his confidence, and so have we. His confidence was that God had done it before – read verses 1-3. He looks back at God's previous dealings with his wayward people and he says, 'Restore us again' (verse 4). He is asking God to do it again – to do for this generation what the Lord had done for their forefathers.

This encourages us to familiarise ourselves with church history. To read of the great revivals of the past, not as an exercise in nostalgia, but to feed our vision of God and to foster a confidence in the grace and care of God for his people.

11.
Why has there not been revival for so long?

James Buchanan said of revival, 'It properly consists in two things – a general impartation of new life and vigour and power to those who are already of the number of God's people; and a remarkable awakening and conversion of souls who hitherto have been careless and unbelieving; in other words, it consists of a new spiritual life imparted to the dead, and a new spiritual health imparted to the living.'[1]

Revival has nothing to do with national temperament or characteristics. It comes to both the stayed English lands and to the more excitable Celtic and Latin countries. In his book *The Flaming Tongue*, Dr Edwin Orr traces revivals in the first half of the 20th century. He takes us to Wales, England, Korea, Scandinavia, Europe, North America, Latin America, Australia, South Africa, India, China and Japan.

Revival is a worldwide phenomenon that knows no boundaries. It touches the very fabric of society and not just the religious scene. Orr says of the 19th Century revival in Britain – 'Revived Evangelicals mobilised opinion and tackled many social injustices, supported modern trade unions and legislated reform of working conditions. None of this was accomplished by force – all of it by verbal persuasion against which the reactionaries could not stand, even though they resisted strenuously. Along with prevention of social injustice came a multitude of agencies created to care for the unfortunate, until at last the very State itself, the still unregenerate society, began adopting the standards of the New Testament as the norm of civilisation.'

He goes on to say, 'Great Britain was the first of the countries of the world to be industrialised, and its workers were caught in a treadmill of competitive drudgery which kept them straining full sixteen hours a day. Evangelical leaders, including Shaftesbury and members of the Clapham Sect, brought about an end to much of the sorry exploitation and promoted all sorts of social improvements. No less an authority than Prime Minister Lloyd George credited to the Evangelical Revival the movement "which improved the condition of the working classes in wages, hours of labour and otherwise." This was paralleled in the United States by what have been called 'Sentimental Years' when organised good works and betterment flourished in the American States.'[2]

In recent years parts of South America and China have experienced remarkable demonstrations of revival power.

This is also true of several Asian countries but not Western Europe. We have to ask ourselves why so many developed countries, such as Britain, the USA, Australia or South Africa, can only look back at these events in history instead of them being part of our present experience?

In Great Britain, for example, we have seen nothing of revival power for a very long time. At the end of the 1940s there was revival in the Hebrides and before that in 1904-05 in Wales, but, for a general revival that touched the whole of Britain, we have to go back to 1859. In January of that year Charles Spurgeon said, 'We must confess that, just now, we have not the outpouring of the Holy Spirit that we could wish.., Oh, if the Spirit of God should come upon those assembled to-night, and upon all the assemblies of the saints, what an effect would be produced. We seek not for extraordinary excitements, those spurious attendants of genuine revivals, but we do seek for the pouring out of the Spirit of God… The Spirit is blowing upon our churches now with His genial breath, but it is as a soft evening gale. Oh, that there would come a rushing mighty wind, that should carry everything before it. This is the lack of the times, the great want of our country. May this come as a blessing from the Most High.'[3] By the end of that year revival had come.

There are no doubt many reasons why revival seems to have disappeared off the religious scene, but I want to suggest three, which I believe, cover the rest.

□ (1) A change in evangelical thinking

It is a simple fact of history that up to the middle of the 19th Century revivals were fairly frequent in Britain. Dr. Eifion Evans says, 'Between 1762 and 1862 there were at least fifteen outstanding revivals in Wales.' But since then Wales has only seen one revival. Why is this?

In those days Christians thought in terms of revival. If there was a period of spiritual drought and things were not well in the church the leaders immediately called the people to prayer and repentance. They cried to God for a visitation of the Holy Spirit. We have seen this in the above words of Spurgeon. The same was true in America. Eifion Evans tells us, 'On 1 December a three-day Convention was called at Pittsburgh under Presbyterian auspices to consider "the necessity for a general revival of religion in all the churches represented and others as well." Charles Hodge preached at the opening session of this Convention on Zechariah 4:6. "This is the word of the Lord unto Zerubbabel saying. Not by might, nor by power, but by my spirit, saith the Lord of hosts." In the sessions which followed; the matters discussed included, firstly, the need for a religious awakening; secondly, hindrances to this; and thirdly, means to be exercised to secure such a blessing.'[4]

That sort of call is rarely heard today. The end of the 19th century saw the rise of liberal theology and Christians faced attacks on the Bible and on the supernatural power of God. It is surely significant that 1859 was the year of the last general revival in Britain and also the year that Charles Darwin's *The Origin of the Species* was published. This

book exploded the theory of evolution in the land and left
the churches in confusion. Evolution caused many nomi-
nal Christians to lose what little faith they had, and it caused
many true Christians to begin to question the truth of the
supernatural power of God. A result of this was that in times
of spiritual darkness, instead of looking, as previous
generations had done, for an intervention of God in
revival they sought to provide the answer themselves. There
arose evangelistic campaigns which were relatively
unknown before this.

Many have been converted through campaigns and they
certainly have their place in church life – but they are no
answer to spiritual drought. The second half of the 20th
century saw an unparalleled number of evangelistic
campaigns in Britain, but at the beginning of the 21st
century the land is more godless than ever.

The thinking of Christians has changed. They do not
pray for revival and do not expect it. Instead we call a com-
mittee, invite an evangelist and organise publicity. That,
by and large, is today's situation and it leads to the second
reason.

☐   (2) Christians do not believe revival is possible

This has become the general view among evangelicals.
Revival has gone out of fashion. We have never experienced it so the tendency is to think that it was possible 100
years ago but not now. The thinking is that our days are
different, people are better off and more educated so that

what moved our forefathers has no effect now. But this forgets that revival is a supernatural activity of God.

In Malachi 3:10 God makes a promise to his people in a time of great spiritual drought, '...see if I will not throw open the floodgates of heaven and pour out so much blessing that you will not have room enough for it.' The context makes it clear that Israel's problem was not agricultural but spiritual. Their whole relationship to God was wrong. The phrase 'floodgates of heaven' (NIV), or 'windows of heaven' (AV) is significant. It is used very rarely in Scripture and each time depicts an extraordinary activity of God.

In Genesis 7:11, the floodgates of heaven were opened to demonstrate the wrath of God in the Flood.

In Malachi 3:10, the floodgates being opened would bring extraordinary blessing.

In 2 Kings 7:2 we read the phrase again. Here is a reaction of unbelief on the lips of an ungodly man. The promise of God (7:1) was ridiculed as being impossible and in our terminology it is equivalent to 'if pigs could fly'. But the impossible happened and did so by divine intervention. God did it.

This is the answer to those who believe that revival is impossible. God can intervene. Malachi believed this, and the glory and power of God is our reason for also believing in revival. The Lord, who has done it before, can do it again. In the first century he turned the world upside down through the preaching of a handful of uneducated men. In the 18th century he turned England upside down through the preaching of George Whitfield – an innkeeper's son from Gloucester, and through the preaching of John Wesley – a somewhat aloof and intellectual Anglican.

☐   (3) Many Christians are afraid of revival

From our safe, calm, tranquil, comfortable port of evangelicalism we view the white-hot fervour of revival with fear. Prayer meetings lasting all night and men crying out in agonies of conviction are all so different from what we know. We fear and talk of too much emotionalism. No one wants carnal emotionalism but we must be careful not to allow the devil to use this fear to cause us to quench the Spirit. Some equate revival with Pentecostalism or charismatic fervour, and say this is not what we want. This merely reveals an ignorance of church history. Nearly every revival in Britain and the USA has come in and through strong Calvinistic circles.

Perhaps the greatest fear is the cost to ourselves. Revival strips away all pride and hypocrisy and reveals secret sins long hidden away.

Brian Edwards writes, 'Revival is always a revival of holiness. And it begins with a terrible conviction of sin. It is often the form that this conviction of sin takes that troubles those who read of revival. Sometimes the experience is crushing. People weep uncontrollably, and worse! But there is no such thing as a revival without tears of conviction and sorrow.'

Edwards goes on to say, 'But all this is only the beginning. Duncan Campbell declared again and again that true revival is a revival of holiness and that holiness is more desirable than happiness. One man, converted under the preaching of Campbell, claimed that his conversion cost him $10,000; he had to return to America and work for a year to make restitution for things he had done as a sinner.'[5]

200 years earlier, the great American theologian Jonathan Edwards commented that one effect of revival is to bring sinners 'immediately to quit their sinful practices'. This deep work of conviction always leads to a freedom and joy in the newfound experience of forgiveness. Following the 'smiting of the heart' come the 'outbursts of the joy of salvation'.

Such happenings are so foreign to our experience that fear is perhaps to be expected. We need to realise that these things are not organised but in revival they are normal. The sense of the Holy Spirit is so real, love for Jesus so precious, an awareness of the holiness of God so intense, that sin cannot remain hidden. Our fears must be taken to God so that we, with saints of previous centuries, can cry to God for revival.

I am not suggesting that if we put these things right we will see revival next week. But I am saying is that we must put these things right or we will never see revival. Reformation is our business but God alone can revive.

12.
What can be

The psalmist wanted to see God's glory in the land and the Lord promised Solomon that he would heal the land. With a God like ours the possibilities of **what can be** are limitless. An Old Testament verse that should encourage us greatly in difficult years is Joel 2:25, 'I will repay you for the years the locusts have eaten...' The theological and moral locusts have been busy in our land, eating away at all that is honourable and true. But when all seems hopeless God can change the scene, and he can do it quickly. The Scriptures and church history bear witness to this.

The book of Joel makes it clear that the problems the people of God were facing were the result of their sin. The swarms of locusts were God's judgement – '...my great army that I sent among you' (2:25). Our God is a God of providence. By the 'providence of God' we mean the unceasing activity of God working in the affairs of men and women. He upholds, guides and governs all events and circumstances, and providence is a direct consequence of divine sovereignty. God is King over all his creation, doing just what he wants. He '...works everything in conformity with the purposes of his will' (Ephesians 1:11). Throughout history there have been various views as to how the world is governed. For instance, deism believed in a remote creator, a god who set the world in motion, but who now stands apart from it like a spectator. Other views see chance or fate as the governing factors. Over against these the Bible teaches that all history is under God's providence. There is a good example of God changing things in Jeremiah 32.

Jeremiah was in prison because he persisted in declaring that God was going to judge Judah and deliver them to the Babylonians. Zedekiah the king did not want to hear of God's judgement and providence. He particularly did not like being told, '...If you fight against the Babylonians, you will not succeed' (v. 5). At this point the prophet was instructed by God to buy a field which belonged to his cousin. He obeyed and the legal transaction was meticulously carried out (vv. 11-12), but in the circumstances the whole thing seemed so pointless. If the enemy were going to capture the land what was the use of buying a field? The point was that God said, '...Houses, fields and vineyards will again be bought in this land' (v.15). Jeremiah was no doubt somewhat confused, but nevertheless he trusted God and obeyed.

Having obeyed, he prays in verses 16-25. The prayer is illuminating. Here is a man with a great view of the sovereignty of God (vv. 17-19). He sees God moving nations in order to bless his people (vs. 20-22). He sees God punishing this blessed people because of their sin (v. 23). In fact, he sees God at work in everything and it is all done for a purpose (v. 24). But it is evident in verse 25 that he is still confused: 'The city is going to be lost, but you say buy the field and have the transaction witnessed.'

Now look at God's answer in verse 27. Here is a declaration of God's sovereignty. He controls the world. The rain falls and the sun shines at his command. Men live and move and breathe only because of God's grace. He is Lord and King and nothing is too hard or impossible for him. We need to be reminded of this. Jeremiah knew it and voiced it in verse 17: '...Nothing is too hard for you,' he said. Then God challenged him in verse 27: He asks Jeremiah [do you really believe what you have said] '...Is anything too hard for me?'

All too often our thoughts of God can be high and correct but only theoretical. Is our doctrine of the sovereignty of God a theory or do we believe it? The providence of God brings us down to earth with a bump, takes divine sovereignty out of the realm of theological theory and reveals it to be completely realistic and practical. God is sovereign and does control (see v. 42). The whole business of buying the field was to show this (vv. 43-44). In a world of uncertainty and confusion, the doctrine of the providence of God should thrill the heart of the Christian.

Even though at times circumstances may deny it. God is in control. We are not leaves blown around by the winds of chance and fate but the children of God held fast in providential hands.

☐ Expectation

There is nothing more important in the Christian life than our understanding of who God is. This will govern everything we do, particularly our sense of expectancy. Take, for instance, the promise in Isaiah 43:2. There God is promising that in the fires of affliction and the waters of sorrow, he will be with us to ensure that these struggles do not overwhelm us. The Lord made that promise 2,700 years ago, but is it relevant to us today? Do we believe, and expect that God can still minister like this to us? Do we believe that God is still God?

Every evangelical Christian would without hesitation say 'Yes. We are believers. We believe the Bible. We believe God will bless us.' But is Tozer right when he wrote, 'We are believers and we can quote the creed with approval. We believe it, but we believe that God will bless some other people, some other place, some other time – but not now, not here and not us.' This basically is our problem. To quote Tozer again, 'If we allow the gloomy voice of unbelief to whisper to us that God will bless some other time but not now, some other place but not here, some other people but not us, we might as well turn off the lights because nobody will get anywhere.'[1]

However, there is another voice calling for our attention. The voice of faith tells us that God means what he says. What he did, he can still do. God is still the same God as he was in Bible times.'

Which voice do we listen to? The answer to this question will determine the sort of Christian lives we live. It will determine the depth of our Christian experience and the breadth of our vision and expectancy.

Faith is most reasonable. It is not a step into the dark but a step out of the dark into the light of God. It hears the promise of God, believes it and trusts God. It is the character of God that makes faith so reasonable.

In his remarkable book *Out of the Rut, into Revival*, A. W. Tozer says, 'What God has ever done for anyone He will do for anybody else. Let us get a hold of this and not write the lives of our fathers and gild the sepulchre of the ones who have gone before, imagining that we live in a vacuum, void of those who have experienced God. Anything God ever did for anyone in faith he will do for anyone else who meets his conditions.

'When God speaks His mighty voice thunders down the years. He speaks to His people called Israel and He speaks to His people called Christians. Nothing has happened to invalidate His promises. We must remember that. Nothing in history would invalidate the promises of God. Nothing in philosophy, nothing that science has ever discovered can invalidate His promises. Certainly there have been social changes, and people look at things differently now than they did in other times. Nevertheless, nothing changes God, His promises, human nature, God's purposes or His intentions toward His people, so we can take the Word of God and say, "Here is a living Word."'[1]

References

Chapter 1 – Then and Now

1 J. Blanchard, *Gathered Gold*, (Kevan), Evangelical Press, 1984, p.182

2 A. W. Tozer, *Root of the Righteous*, Christian Publications, 1955, p.49-50

Chapter 2 – Worship

1 (John Bunyan), A. P. Davis, Issac Watts, Independent Press, 1948, p.195

2 S. M. Houghton, *Sketches from Church History*, Banner of Truth, p.185-6

3 J. Frame, *Contemporary Worship Music*, P&R, 1997, p.15-16

Chapter 7 – Where do we go from here?

1 A. W. Tozer, *The Price of Neglect*, Christian Publications, 1991, p.6

2 J. Brown, *Discourses*, Banner of Truth, Vol. 3, 1967, p, 88

3   D. M. Lloyd-Jones, *Walking with God*, Crossway, 1995, p.57
4   J. M. Boice, *Ephesians: An Expositional Commentary*, Zonderman, 1988, p.50
5   D. M. Lloyd-Jones, *Walking with God*, Crossway, 1995, p.60-61
6   (Erasmus Saunders) L. T. Davies, *Welsh Life in the 18th Century*, Country Life, 1937, p.5

Chapter 9 – Dealing with problems in the church

1   S. Ollyott, *Alive in Christ*, Evangelical Press, 1994, p.97
2   J. M. Boice, *Ephesians: An Expositional Commentary*, Zonderman, 1988, p.118

Chapter 10 – Revival

1   M. Roberts, *Banner Magazine*, August 1990
2   B. H. Edwards, *Revival*, Evangelical Press, 1994, p.26

Chapter 11 – Why has there been no revival for so long?

1   J. Buchanan, *The office and work of the Holy Spirit*, Banner of Truth, 1966, p. 227
2   E. Orr, *The Flaming Tongue*, Moody, 1973, p.xi-xii
3   C. H. Spurgeon, *Revival Year Sermons*, Banner of Truth, p.9
4   E. Evans, *When He is Come*, EMW, 1959, p.27
5   B. Edwards, *Revival*, Evangelical Press, p.115 & 121

Chapter 12 – What can be

1   A. W. Tozer, *Out of the Rut into Revival*, Hodder, 1993, p.151-3

Other books by Peter Jeffery distributed by Evangelical Press

- *Bitesize theology* – An ABC of the Christian faith

- *Christian handbook* – A guide to the Bible, church history and Christian doctrine

- *Enjoying God always* – 366 daily devotions

- *Following the shepherd* – The 23rd Psalm

- *How shall they hear?* – Church-based evangelism

- *How to behave in church* – A guide to church life

- *Lights shining in the darkness* – Introducing some of the great men of faith

- *The Lord's Supper* – Important questions that many ask about this ordinance

- *Opening up Ephesians* – A young people's guide into the glorious book of Ephesians

- *Our present sufferings* – Helpful to Christians who are going through a time of suffering

- *Overcoming life's difficulties* – Learning from the book of Joshua

- *Rainbow of grace* – Learning from the life of Noah

- *Salvation exposed* – God's way of salvation

- *Seeking God* – A clear explanation of how to find God

- *Sickness and death in the Christian family* – Rest and encouragement in God in times of stress and loss

- *Stand firm* – A young Christians' guide to the armour of God

- *Struggling but winning* – A survival guide for Christians

- *Walk worthy* – Guidelines for Christian life

- *What you need to know about salvation* – A day-by-guide to the Christian faith

- *Which way to God?* – A full-colour presentation of the gospel for giving away

- *You can't fool God* – The greatest delusion of all is to believe there is no God

- *The young Spurgeon* – Spurgeon's early years and first experience of preaching

A wide range of excellent books on spiritual subjects is available from Evangelical Press. Please write to us for your free catalogue or contact us by e-mail.

Evangelical Press
Faverdale North Industrial Estate, Darlington, DL3 OPH, England

Evangelical Press USA
PO Box 84, Auburn, MA 01501, USA

e-mail sales: sales@evangelicalpress.org

web: http://www.evangelicalpress.org